God's
Shining Jewels

Marvin and Helen Frey

God's
Shining Jewels

Marvin and Helen Frey

ISBN 13:978-1-59581-431-9
ISBN 10:1-59581-431-0

Cover based on poster calligraphy
designed by Timothy R. Botts

Published in the United States of America by:
BRENTWOOD CHRISTIAN PRESS
WWW.BRENTWOODBOOKS.COM
1-800-334-8861

Table of Contents

Dedication

I dedicate this book to the Lord, Jesus Christ. His Spirit has inspired Marvin and me to share with others the wealth of experiences God has brought into our lives and ministry in forty-five years of service to Christ and the youth of New York City. In memory of my dear husband, Marvin V. Frey.

* * * * *

"This is my commandment, that ye love one another, as I have loved you." John 15:12

* * * * *

Acknowledgements

To our extended family, Tom and Esther Gajtkowski. To the Board of Trustees for their faithful leadership and support through the forty-five years' ministry. To the countless number of friends and supporters, without whom the Children's Fund of New York, Inc. would not have been possible. To Mrs. Vicki deVries, who has faithfully guided me to the book's completion.

Introduction

In writing this book, it was Marvin's strong desire that some readers who sense a definite call from God to start a children's and youth ministry in the Inner-City would be strengthened in their faith, and encouraged to say 'yes' to such a call. Marvin's call came after a long period of heart searching prayer, through a vision from God, in which he saw many unloved children on the streets of New York City. Marvin knew without question that this was what God wanted him to do with his life.

For about ten years, there were fears and doubts crossing Marvin's mind, the enemy trying to dissuade him from his call. His strength was gone, but there was nothing wrong with him when a doctor examined him. Then his final answer to God came, "All right, Lord, I'll go to New York City, if I have to walk across the country." Some months prior to his arrival in New York City, God blessed him with meetings across the country, from Portland, Oregon to New York City.

Our involvement in the lives of thousands of children and youth on the Lower East Side of Manhattan, for forty-five years has been a humbling, yet rewarding experience, and one we would not exchange for anything in the world. To God be all the glory for His great grace and love.

1
Growing Up

I suspect that few who have known me over the years would have considered me "ordinary," although few who knew me in my youth would have called me "exceptional." I was taller and skinnier than most of my peers. Compared to my brothers I was hardly athletic. As a student I struggled to maintain average grades. A poor diet in my early childhood left me with deficiencies that weakened my bones and spoiled my teeth. But I believe that one thing I developed early in my life that more than compensated for these and other so-called deficiencies was faith and commitment to God. From my youth on, I have sincerely believed that God has had a destiny for my life and that, by God's power at work within me, I can literally do anything that God assigns me to do.

I was born in 1918, the fourth of 12 children (nine boys and three girls), to Charles and Anna Frey in Sherwood, Oregon. My parents were devout Christians and strict parents whose own parents were German immigrants. My father, Charles Frey, was a builder who had built his own spacious suburban Portland home overlooking three spectacular mountain peaks: Mt. St. Helen's, Mt. Adams, and Mt. Hood.

While my parents held their Christian faith in common, their approaches to that faith were clearly different. My father held to a strong Pentecostal viewpoint and participated in the ministry of a Pentecostal Mission in Portland. My mother, on the other hand, wanting us children to have a solid Sunday school experience and be taught important Bible truths, took us to a German Baptist church. The difference in their approaches to their faith was cause for some significant tension in our home.

Having attended church and Sunday school throughout my childhood, I made my own decision to become a follower of Jesus Christ at the age of 12. Responding to an invitation from the pulpit, during an evening service at The First German Baptist Church, I walked forward to make a public profession of Christ and was prayed for by the pastor's wife.

I half expected some unusual feeling of joy, happiness and peace, but I felt none of this. Although a little disappointed, I reasoned within myself, *Why should I feel any special sort of happiness?* I had not been sad. As for peace, I was not really a troubled person, as the preachers sometimes described in their sermons. What I had done was to take my stand as a Christian. I simply believed.

Then, when I returned to my seat, I felt something that has never left me. I felt confidence. I felt confident that I had done the right thing and that made me feel good. I had arrived at this conclusion intellectually, but now it affected my whole being, my whole life. Yes, confidence is the word that described my feeling and my attitude at that moment. I had confidence in God's purpose for my life. I had confidence in myself as a person. I had confidence in God's redemption through Christ. To this day, confidence is still the word that best describes my total attitude toward life, religion and the future.

My confidence in myself, in God and in many of the things that young people typically take for granted, was put to a severe test in the year that I turned 15.

2
High School Glory Days

As a youth I was tall and thin. Not overly strong or well coordinated; but, I still enjoyed sports and was one of the fastest runners in my school. This skill not only enabled me to win a number of foot races, but also made me a good choice to play an end position on the school football team. I was fast enough to break into the clear and receive a pass for a potentially significant gain in yardage. Unfortunately, my body was a victim of milk rationing when I was an infant at the end of World War I. As well as having to put up with defective tooth enamel, I lived with a constant fear of bone injuries, each one of which I felt severely.

A moment of potential glory for me as a football player turned to catastrophe in the final seconds of a tied championship game. I made a wide arc to receive the ball from the quarterback. He completed a pass to me and I streaked for the end zone. I fully expected to score the winning touchdown, but the eleven members of the opposing team had other ideas. All eleven took after me, tackled me and piled on top of me. I heard and felt something crack in the area of my hip, and I realized immediately that something was seriously wrong. I will never forget the thoughts that went through my mind — *I hope I can walk when I get up.* Gradually, the bodies were untangled, and I lay on the ground. I had to be helped off the field and taken home by a friend. From that moment until now I have never been without pain in my hip or leg.

It took some time for me to fully realize how serious an injury I had suffered. I continued with my school work, but found it extremely difficult to get around, first with a cane and then with crutches, which my favorite Aunt Mildred had purchased for me.

My injury went unattended for months because of my father's belief and insistence that prayer could solve anything, including my crippling hip disorder. Pa refused to make a decision to get medical help for me, but eventually granted me the option of making a decision for myself.

"I believe God can do all things," Pa told me. "I believe God can heal you, but if you feel you want to go to the hospital, I will take you."

As a fifteen-year-old boy, I believed, too. The public practice of prayer for the sick was part of the faith of our church, and I had experienced healing as a result of prayer on prior occasions. An abscessed ear had been completely healed after my father had prayed a loud and fervent prayer while clapping his hands over both of my ears. For the first five years of my life, I had been cross-eyed and needed glasses to see clearly. At five years old, I was taken forward during a service at the Mission and all the Pastors on the platform came down and laid hands on me. The event frightened me a bit. A few days later my eyes began to hurt, and I found the pain stopped when I took my glasses off. My eyes were no longer crossed. From that time on, until I needed reading glasses as an older man, I enjoyed 20/20 vision. So far, however, prayer had done nothing to lessen this pain in my hip, nor had it made my walking any easier.

Despite my major discomfort, I was not inclined to baby myself, nor did I receive any sympathy from my schoolmates. In fact, I was sometimes appalled at their cruelty. Getting on board a crowded school bus with crutches, I would be pushed around and seldom given a seat. Although I received similar indifferent or abusive treatment as I negotiated crowded school hallways and stairways, I was determined to go to school. Still, having tried for months to abide by my father's insistence that faith was the answer to my need for healing, I felt that the unceasing pain had become more than I could bear. I was frank with my father, telling him, "We have tried prayer and I'm not any better. I want to find out what is wrong with me."

Up to that time Pa and my Aunt Mildred were engaged in an ongoing argument over my predicament. My father believed until the day he died, not only in divine healing, but in divine health, saying, "By faith, you can keep well." Aunt Mildred was a staunch German Baptist and a registered nurse who urged immediate medical attention. Finally, after one of their heated discussions, my father came to me and asked if I wanted to go to the hospital. He refused to have any part in the decision regarding the surgery. He left it totally up to me, and I felt confident that God did not intend for me to spend the rest of my life in a wheelchair.

I had great respect for my father and genuinely admired his strong faith. I was willing to trust God to heal me, but, like Aunt Mildred, I also believed that God might use doctors in the process. I was eager to find out what was wrong with my hip and my leg, and I asked to go to the hospital.

3
Facing Challenges

Because it was during the depression and my father was trying to support 12 children with whatever carpentry jobs he could find, I had to go to a public hospital. Although not as fine as some private hospitals, its location next to the medical school of the University of Oregon lent it an aura of respect.

The first step in diagnosis was to have X-rays taken, a still relatively crude procedure in the 1930s. I will never forget those big, ugly machines. I sat with my naked body on a cold stone-like slab, and it seemed as if they kept me there forever. They took an unusually large number of pictures of me lying flat, on both sides, standing up, sitting, but the pictures taken that day were not sufficient, thus necessitating another visit to the X-ray room.

A few days later, the surgeon, considered one of the best bone specialists in the Northwest, came with the news that an operation would be required. As skilled as he was, he could not assure me that the surgery would accomplish the goal of enabling me to walk unaided. He said the chances of success in that regard were 50-50. "The operation may fail," he admitted.

I had not lost my faith in God, and, in lieu of my father's willingness to take responsibility for a decision; I gave my approval for the operation.

When the operation was completed, I was returned to my hospital room in a cast that encased me from my chest to my toes. I was told I must lie perfectly still, that I must not move or stretch for a period of three to four weeks. Although I tended to be conservative when it came to physical activity, for a 15-year-old boy to be confined without any movement was pure torture. The first couple of days were the most difficult I believe I ever spent.

It would be six torturous months before I would be released from my chest-to-toe cast. The monotony was only slightly relieved by limited interaction with my roommates, who included one old man who boisterously voiced his dislike for the young and complained to everyone about being "stuck in a room with a skinny little kid." My attempts to be nice to him were never accepted.

My only real solace came via a radio that my family had given to me. It became my contact with the outside world. I especially enjoyed a daily Christian program called "The Haven of Rest." The smooth professionalism of 'First Mate Bob,' the sincerity that was vocally evident, the selection of his material and the fine music — all captivated me. And the music was superb, including a fine organ with an organist that could not be topped and the best male quartet that I have ever heard. This daily broadcast became my daily church. Everything I did was timed for this broadcast. And now, several decades later, I can remember how time stood still while the "Haven of Rest" was on the air.

Another of my frustrations during my long months of hospital confinement was the lapse in my formal education. At that time, the Portland City School District made no effort to help children like me to keep up with their schooling. I inquired about it, but got only evasive replies. From my childhood, I have always been an avid newspaper reader, and I had read numerous statements from school officials, such as, "It is our duty to give our children the best education possible; the latest learning methods; the finest textbooks; the most qualified teachers." Yet I had not had one visit in six months from anybody in the Portland School

District. They hadn't even sent me one book to read. I did get library books from the book cart that went through the hospital, thanks to the person in charge of books who always saw that I had plenty of reading material.

After I expressed these concerns to my surgeon, he also saw to it that I got good reading material. In addition, I pored through my grandfather's vast collection (he had collected 30 years' worth) of *National Geographic* magazines, which he graciously shared with me.

Over the course of six months I could sense no improvement in my condition, only increased pain in my hip. Finally, the doctor ordered the cast to be cut off. My enjoyment of the delicious feeling of lying in bed freed from my plaster prison was soon replaced by a wave of depression as it became evident that I would be unable to walk. The operation had failed. My leg and hip would no longer support the weight of my body in any way.

Following several more weeks of waiting and more X-rays, the famous surgeon came to my room to talk to me. His somewhat artificial attempts to raise my morale were ineffective. Finally, he came to the point. Another operation was necessary, involving a new process with new techniques.

From what he was trying to tell me, I understood that the chances of success were still only 50-50. The prospect of spending another eight months in the hospital was an unbearable thought, but I realized I was confronting a decision that was crucial to my future and to my ability to walk again.

"Shall I walk again?" I asked the surgeon.

"The only chance is to operate."

"But you failed the first time."

His face saddened, and he replied, "I know, but it was hard to keep you still."

I said, "Well, I tried to keep still."

He said this operation would be different and he tried to explain what would happen. He noted that, even if the operation was successful, I would still only have partial use of my hip.

"That would be better than no use at all,' I said. "Let me think about it overnight."

The surgeon felt I could live through the operation, but, because of my weakened condition after six months of inactivity, he wasn't totally hopeful on that score either.

I slept little and prayed all night. Toward morning I felt peace come over me and I went to sleep. In the morning I said, "It's okay. I'll have the operation."

This operation was more difficult. I lost a lot of blood, which required a series of hasty transfusions in the middle of the night. My older brother, William, donated the blood. I lay in a coma for days.

When I awoke, it was the middle of the night. The Lord was bringing me to a decision truly to serve Him, but I was deeply troubled inside. Eight months in the hospital, an angry old man in the next bed who took every opportunity to be nasty to me—this was unlike any experience I had ever had before. Away from home and mother for so long: would I ever see my family again? Would I ever be home again?

In my weakness, I could hardly move my fingers. I had reached bottom and felt myself slipping into numbness. I knew death was near. I called out to the Lord with all my strength, "Lord, Help me! Lord, save me! I'll serve you wherever you want me to go."

At that moment I was filled with peace, and I went to sleep immediately. I woke up a few days later, weak but recovering. My pastor and other Christians had visited me during that time and had prayed for me. I began to mend and feel strength coming into my body. My recovery was rapid.

4
Healing Begins

As my body began to mend, I gained strength and began making contacts with other long-term patients in the hospital. At the same time, my faith for my own healing was also becoming stronger, and I prayed sincerely, believing that I would be healed.

The doctor had said I would be in the cast for eight months. After only six weeks I felt ready to get out of the cast and began asking to be let out. I talked to the surgeon, who, in turn, talked to my parents. My father again said it was my decision, but they would stand behind me.

The surgeon—a Methodist— came to me and talked at length about divine healing. His objection was not about healing from God, but his venom was poured out primarily upon certain famous divine healing evangelists. We talked about the nature of faith. Yes, he believed in the virgin birth of Christ and that Christ is the savior of the world. He also believed that God had given man medical skill and knowledge and that we should use that to our advantage. I agreed with him, but I said, "When that advantage puts me in bed without the possibility of walking, what then? Are you going to let me lie here without any hope?"

"Well," he said, "that's the only hope I can give you, that your body will mend and that the operation will have been successful." At what point, he could not tell, but he would not let the cast be taken off. In two weeks, he came back to see how I was progressing. My attitude had not changed, nor had his. He left for another two weeks.

There were doctors who visited us every day, but the surgeon only came around occasionally to check on his patients' progress. I finally talked one of the other doctors into taking my cast off. He was doing it for research.

"I'm not interested in whether or not you are going to walk; I am just interested in what is going to happen to you," he admitted candidly.

Although this was something of a cold-blooded attitude, it pleased me, as it gave me an opportunity to tell the surgeon I had someone who would take off the cast. The large, heavy cast was down both of my legs. I could not move a muscle.

Finally, after about three months, the surgeon said, "Well, it's not something I will approve, but I'm not going to stand in your way, either. It is to be totally your decision."

My parents had to sign release papers stipulating that, in the event something serious should develop, they could not sue the surgeon. Within a week, I had recruited a team— a doctor, an intern and a nurse—to execute the cast's removal. Finally, the big day arrived.

It was a beautiful day. The sun was shining, and as it came through the windows of my solarium room, I said, "Thank you, Lord, for this beautiful day in which you are going to show the world you are still healing people today."

The doctor came in, accompanied by the intern and the nurse, with big shears. I have never seen any quite that large. Snip, snip, snip they went—cold steel against my flesh—as they cut that cast off. An hour later the cast was off. I felt free! I thanked the doctor and his staff, and the doctor said to me, "Young man, God has given you an extra measure of faith and I am praying for you, too." The others remained silent. I lay there on the bed, just feeling the sensation of clean sheets, a delicious feeling I remember clearly to this day.

Although my surgeon was not due for a visit for several days, he came to see me the following day and asked my permission to examine me. He warned me to go slow in my efforts to use my hip again, reminding me that I had been in bed for over a year.

Then he said to me, "I know God answers prayer and especially the prayers of the young and innocent, and I know He will not forget you, Marvin. I cannot have that kind of faith, but I believe God will answer your prayer." He was in tears when he left the room.

It was ten days before I felt strong enough to push my feet over to the side of the bed. Regaining the use of my legs involved a regimen that I set for myself. Nobody advised or aided me in this matter. I decided I would start by sitting up for a period of time daily for a few days, then progress to spending time standing by my bed for a few days, then move onto walking around the bed.

For a week, I spent an hour sitting up with my feet dangling over the side of the bed in the morning and another hour in the afternoon. I was also pushing my feet against the bedstead, getting them used to the feeling of weight.

On my first try at standing up, I discovered that my legs would not support the weight of my body, and I fell back on the bed. However, I kept trying two or three times a day until I could stand up straight, fully supporting my weight without leaning on anything. This was another week's progress. Then, holding onto the bed, I attempted to walk around it. On my third or fourth try I made it all the way around. I got back into bed weak and tired. I was in tears but extremely happy.

Progress was accelerated from that moment on. I still could not walk without support, but I could get from my bed into a wheelchair. Immediately, I began visiting friends in other wards. They had exchanged notes for months, and patients from throughout the floor had been kept abreast of every step in my progress. As I wheeled myself into their rooms and wards, I received a hearty cheer, applause and handshakes all around.

I knew God was helping me in some miraculous way, but it had been an effort of faith on my part. Each step that I took required the greatest amount of faith, and God did not fail me. As I prepared to leave the hospital, I was presented with a walker, which helped me stand on my feet.

Before I left for home, the surgeon told me, "Your rapid recovery and your ability to walk so quickly after that very serious operation can only be the work of God. Your faith made this possible; not my medical skill. Son, I do not believe in divine healing as your father does. However," he reiterated, "I do believe God answers the prayers of the young and innocent and I know he has answered yours."

The evidence was clear enough. It was a miraculous recovery from an operation for which the surgeon could not assure even a 50-50 chance of success. Although he could not bring himself to believe in God's regular intervention in man's physical problems, he could believe that God would listen to those who will call upon Him with a sincere and earnest heart. The Lord heard me and miraculously healed me.

5

A Touch From The Lord

More of the miracle still lay ahead. Although I left the hospital walking, I still needed the support of crutches. At least, I was walking, and that made me happy. I took the surgeon's suggestions seriously and tried to avoid putting full weight on my hip. It was months before I was able to return to school.

It was during that time that Raymond T. Richey, a healing evangelist from Texas, came to our home church. Of course, everyone urged me, including my pastor, to be prayed for. Richey waited a whole week before he had a prayer line. He wanted people to be prepared, he said. Finally, I was prayed for. Up to that time, I had not walked without my crutches. I had stood, but I had not walked without them.

Richey was a small man, and I towered over him by a foot. So, he had to reach up when he prayed for me. He laid hands on me and anointed me with oil, at which time my pastor also laid hands on me. His prayer was simple, "Lord, heal this boy." Then he took my crutches and said, "Now, young man, I want you to walk."

I said, "I can't."

"Yes, you can, in faith," he said.

I started to walk, for the first time without my crutches. I do not remember what happened with the crowd, but I was told everything was bedlam for a few moments. That is, they were shouting and praising the Lord for what they had just witnessed. I walked across the platform and down the steps, and everyone was smiling at me as I made my way back to my seat. My mother and brothers were smiling with tears running down their cheeks. Strangely, I did not experience any unusual feeling, except that I felt stronger. There was no great surge of power, only a slight tingling that I felt when Mr. Richey touched me. It was the Lord, and the Lord had healed me because now I was walking without crutches.

As I sat watching the rest of the service, I looked back at the sets of stairs on either side of the platform. On one side stood elders of the church helping the crippled and aged up the stairs. Others stood by the other steps to help those who had been prayed for to get down. When I had walked away from Mr. Richey toward those downward steps, I did not want any help going down. Although I had moved slowly, I had succeeded in descending the six narrow steps unaided, even though there was not so much as a railing to steady me. The miracle took on a new dimension as I realized that now I would be capable of ascending the steps to the second floor of my parents' home—where my room was—without difficulty.

Fully accepting my new status, as an unaided walker, did not come easily. I had become so used to depending on my crutches for security that I hated to give them up; so, I had left them at the altar. Furthermore, my Aunt Mildred had given them to me and had told me she would like me to return them to her when I was through with them.

I asked my mother to take me down to the tent. She parked the car in front of the tent and I walked around, amazed at how strong I was. I knew that they kept the discarded crutches and canes in the back. As I was about to open the flap of the tent, the Lord spoke to me in a voice that I could hear audibly.

"What are you doing here, Marvin?"

I was surprised but I knew it was the voice of the Lord. "Lord, I'm here to get my crutches," I said.

He replied, "Well, I healed you, didn't I?"

That stopped me. "Yes, Lord, You healed me." And I stood there for the longest time, trying to decide what to do. Finally, I turned around and walked back to the car. My mother asked me if I had found them and I said, "No." She started up the car and we drove home. She didn't say a word, but I knew that she had been praying the whole time.

6
Playing Catch-Up

Although I had experienced a miracle that enabled me to walk unaided, like Jacob who had wrestled with the angel of the Lord, I would walk with a limp and some pain for the rest of my life. As a result, I walked more slowly than my peers when I returned to school, and this caused me some consternation.

At school I had all kinds of stairs to maneuver and, with the onrush of students, it was very difficult to get from one room to the next. Having to negotiate the stairs slowed me down so that I could not help being late for class and was often marked late. The experience caused me to have some bitter feelings.

Although I could hardly have been considered a "rebel," I was not always comfortable with conforming to expectations merely for the sake of appeasing others. I was also far more interested in the flow of life around me than I was in pure academic pursuits. Consequently, despite a fairly high level of intelligence and my voracious reading habits (I read virtually every book in our school's library!), I did not shine as an exemplary student as my older siblings did. Part of the problem was based in the expectation of educators in those days, who often prized conformity and rote responses far above innovative thinking from their pupils.

I was always outshone by my brothers and sisters. James, the eldest, was granted a four-year, all-expenses-paid scholarship to the "Harvard of the West," Stanford University, the only one Stanford gave that year. He graduated from Portland's prestigious Benson's Polytechnic. Henrietta, David and John were all straight-A students, and then I came along with an occasional B, a rare A, mostly C's. Once in a while, I bumped down to an F. I was on the bottom rung of the educational ladder and I knew it. I just wasn't as smart as they were at school work. They always did what the teacher told them, but I preferred to look out the window and watch the wind blow through the trees. Nature always fascinated me. I found a common spirit at school in a couple of teachers—the music and art teachers—who seemed excited about my talents in those areas.

It was while I was still in high school that I began to manifest some special talents in music, setting the stage for a ministry in music that would come to have a far-ranging impact. After a minimum of formal training as a pianist, I worked diligently to teach myself to become an accomplished gospel pianist. Although I had a genuine appreciation for classical music, I made a conscious choice to devote myself to the gospel genre as a vehicle for serving my Lord.

Finding it difficult to practice my piano playing at home, amid a houseful of unappreciative siblings, I received permission to practice on the piano in the basement of my home church and did so most days after school. It was on that piano, in 1935, at the age of 17, in the midst of a personal sacrifice, that I composed my first chorus, "I Have a Jubilee Down in My Heart."

I had been asked to take a lead part in a high school musical in which I would sing a popular Cole Porter song called "Jubilee." However, my church, the Four-Square Church of Portland, forbade me to accept the part since it was in a secular show. When I told the teacher who had offered me the part, she berated me and told me I would never get anywhere in music unless I would sing the music people sing.

As I went to the church basement to practice on the piano and seek consolation, the song ran through my mind as I said, "Why should I worry? I already have a jubilee down in my heart."

This marked the simple beginning of what was to become the songwriting career by which the Lord would enable me to have some impact upon much of Christendom around the world. Other choruses followed as I, still a teenager, stepped into another powerful ministry as a musician-evangelist.

7
Preacher In Process

As I heard various laymen preach at the Franklin Mission, where I went with my father, I became convinced that I could preach as well as or better than they if given the opportunity. That opportunity came when circumstances prevented another man from fulfilling a preaching assignment, and I was given permission to serve as his replacement. Thus, I preached my first sermon.

How could I forget that experience? Across the street from Mulligan's, a saloon with a block-long bar requiring twenty bartenders, was Franklin's Mission, operated by Frank and Nancy Franklin, an elderly couple who had spent their life running gospel missions in Missouri and other western states. They used a large upstairs loft with an apartment in front. In the center was a chapel that would seat about 125 people. In the back was a kitchen and dining hall, where the men were fed—mostly winos or bums down on their luck, or men in between logging jobs.

These woodsmen worked hard and lived hard lives. They would work for three months in the woods where everything was provided for them except for liquor and women. When their contracts were up, they would return to Portland and head for the closest bar, usually Mulligan's, which was advertised as the longest bar in the world. I once paced off the sidewalk in front, which was 180 feet long.

In those days the streets of the Northwest cities were full of old men who were no longer able to work in the woods due to old age, accelerated by their life of dissipation, no social security and no access to welfare. The only way they could live was by panhandling. Their money usually went for a bottle of cheap wine and a bed in a flophouse. For food they could always depend on a good hardy bowl of soup, four slices of bread, and a mug of coffee at Ma Franklin's Mission, after listening to the service of the evening. If they didn't like her loud and lively music and preaching, they could always go to the Union Mission where they would get two slices of bread and a mug of coffee. Naturally, the more food offered, the more men that came.

The food solicited by Pa Franklin usually came from liquid food businesses. Occasionally, they got a bonus—hot tamales, the balance of an over-run from a nearby tamale shop at Third and Ankeny Streets. These short, fat chicken and beef tamales were the best I have tasted anywhere—in the South, East, or West.

The service was really an experience. Ma Franklin played a mean banjo and Pa Franklin played the drums, when he wasn't stirring the soup. At the piano was a nine-year-old named Buddy, who could pound out the chords but nothing else. It didn't matter, because Ma Franklin had a voice like a shrill foghorn, clear as a bell, so you always knew where you were in the song. The men knew that if they wanted to please Ma Franklin, they would have to sing; so, sing they did, loud and lively, but not always in tune.

Ma had a big heart and would always give help to those she believed needed it. She didn't have much use for the professional panhandlers, and there were lots of them, but there was one she always took time for. I don't remember his name and he never came to the services, but in the middle of the afternoon he would walk up the stairs clanking with every step. He would sit down and talk with Ma Franklin, and he was a real character. He had three overcoats filled with carefully sewn pockets in which he carried all sorts of things—paper, pen, scissors, needle, and thread of various colors, pots and pans, and a grocery list. One time I thought I'd see if he literally had "everything" in those pockets, which it seemed to me he did. I asked him if he had a jar opener. He looked at me, smiled, then opened his three coats, reached into a low pocket, felt around for a few moments and soon put a rusty jar opener on the table. He said he hadn't used it in over a year. With that, he got up, picked up his bread, put it in one of his pockets and strolled out, rattling all the way with his pots and other items.

8
Preaching At The Mission

The Franklin mission services often had special speakers—usually laymen who thought more of their preaching ability than they should have. Most of the members of the audience were too numbed by liquor to really understand what was being preached. Occasionally, when Buddy was absent, I was asked to play the piano and to help in the street meetings with a guitar, a half-hour prior to the service. I teased Ma Franklin for an opportunity to preach, but she considered me at 17 years of age to be too young for that responsibility. Still, I continued to pester her.

Then the opportunity came. A brother who was scheduled to preach could not be there and I was to preach the next Tuesday. I had just four days to prepare my sermon. In prayer in my room, I sought for a text and was given one immediately—John 3:16: "For God so loved the world that He gave his only begotten son, that whosoever believeth on him should not perish but have everlasting life." I frankly told the Lord I didn't want to preach on that text. I wanted to preach on something deeper, not something so elementary—maybe something from St. Paul's letters or from the Old Testament, such as Proverbs. My mind was filled with great gospel sermons I had read and heard and was gathering in books in my library, but the answer came again: John 3:16.

For the next three days, I argued with the Lord, searching for texts throughout the Bible, but each time I would come back in prayer, open my Bible and it would fall open to John 3:16. Some criticize this method of discerning divine guidance, but every time the Bible would open to the same place, John 3:16.

Finally, I made a short outline:

1. For God so loved
2. The world
3. That He gave—God gives
4. His only Son
5. Whoever believes—faith
6. Will not perish—saved from destruction
7. Everlasting life—God's gift of hope

I was nervous, but when it came time to deliver the sermon I was able to follow my outline. The men were polite, but inattentive; they had heard it all before and now from a kid who didn't know what life was all about. At the close, I prayed and gave an invitation to the men to accept Christ, while singing the hymn "Just As I Am."

I hoped that some of the men before me would come forward and make a decision to accept Christ into their hearts. No one stepped forward during the singing of the hymn. I then asked that the first verse be sung again, during which time a middle-aged man came forward. He knelt at the right of the mourners' bench, on the same level as the pulpit. He looked the same as the other bums—dirty, disheveled, wearing a fine cloth coat clearly filthy. I put my arms around him as I knelt beside him, something I had been warned not to do, because of the possibility of vermin. I continued to pray softly, hoping that would lead him into a confession and repentance of sins and his acceptance of Christ as Savior and cleanser from sin. After a few moments I saw a puddle of tears on the bench. I knew something was happening.

Ma Franklin believed in loud vocal repentance. They kept singing, this time one of Ma's loud and fast songs. I got in front of the man, as close as possible, and whispered, "Just ask Jesus to forgive you and to save you. Say this prayer after me, 'Jesus forgive me; Jesus save me.'"

In a few moments he got up, dried his tears, put his hands down and went to his seat without a word. I didn't get his name or learn anything about him. When the service was over, he went along with the other 100 men into the dining room to have soup and bread. I didn't see him after that.

Ma Franklin said, "Well, Marvin, one man came forward. We can be thankful for that." She said nothing about my sermon, although some of the people did compliment me and one even said I might make a pretty good preacher some day.

My next visit to the mission was three nights later. After the service a man came up to me. Neatly dressed, he stood out among the bums. He asked if I remembered him, and I replied, "No, I don't believe I do." He went on, saying he was the man who had knelt at the bench at the close of the service on Tuesday night. I guess I looked amazed. My eyes opened wide, as did my mouth. When I recovered, I said, "Praise the Lord. It seems the Lord did something for you."

He continued, "I went to my bed in the flophouse and couldn't sleep all night. The first thing I did when I got up was to get a bath and clean my clothes." (In the skid row area there were small shops that specialized in these services—baths 75 cents; clothes cleaned and pressed while you wait, five cents. You waited in a little booth while these services were being performed.) "Then I went out and found a job washing dishes."

I asked him what it was that had brought him forward, secretly hoping it had been something in my sermon. He said that after I read John 3:16, he could remember nothing of what I said. His mind had gone back to the first time he heard that Scripture—at his mother's knee.

"While you were preaching, I could think of nothing except all the times I had heard it preached and I had taught it to my children." He said it reminded him of his son, just my age, and when he heard the hymn, "Just As I Am," he could not sit any longer. "The Scripture you read reminded me of my son and some of the awful things I have done to my family and myself. I thank God and thank you, young man, for reading that Scripture, which has changed my life."

I was speechless and in tears, as he was. He shook my hand, holding it momentarily without saying a word; then he said, "God bless you, son," and left the hall.

Ma Franklin came to me at that time and asked if that was the man who had come forward. I replied, "Yes, the Lord saved him and really cleaned him up." Then she had a real shouting time, but by then the man was already down the stairs.

I visited with that man three or four times after that day and learned that he had been a banker in Chicago. He started drinking socially and later more heavily. Subsequently, he lost his job, his home, and his family and the resulting depression had reduced him to the pathetic condition he was in when he walked into Ma Franklin's for the first time, seeking food on the night of my sermon.

One day, three months later, he came to say goodbye, as he was going back to try to find a job and to try for reconciliation with his family. I had counseled him on this. He asked me if I had a father who had done the things he had done to his son, could I forgive him. That was a hard question for me to answer. Even though things between my father and me displeased me, I could never say that my father had abused me or caused me to be in want. I told him that I didn't know, but I had been taught this one thing, that God can do anything. I said I believed that if he prayed and wanted to be re-united with his family, and if he took the right steps in that direction, his family could be reunited.

I didn't hear from this man for four years and then received two letters with no return address, but postmarked Chicago. He had found a job selling insurance and was reunited with his family in a complete reconciliation. The second letter told about his being chosen a deacon in the Methodist church where he and his family were now attending services. John 3:16—the first verse I had ever memorized and the premiere verse in the Bible—not my weak sermon, but the work of the Holy Spirit beyond my understanding had brought the changes in this man, so far away from God. To this day, all I can say is "Praise the Lord."

9

Becoming A
Gospel Musician And Evangelist

Following closely upon the writing of my first chorus, "I Have a Jubilee Down in My Heart," I wrote several others, including "Come By Here," (later translated into an African dialect to become the world-famous "Kum Ba Yah"), "Eternity," "Do Lord," "Let Jesus Fix It for You," and others.

In the summer of my seventeenth year, I was invited to be a speaker and sing a song at a camp meeting in Turner, Oregon, near Salem, featuring Charles S. Price, a well-known evangelist of the time. When the regular pianist had to leave in response to an emergency at home, I was invited to be the pianist, both morning and evening, for the two weeks of revival meetings. I took on challenges that went well beyond merely playing the piano.

The acoustics at the big barn of the tabernacle were horrible. I have never heard worse. Old, drafty, big, with a poor public address system, the building could probably safely accommodate 3,000, and they let in an additional thousand. A group of young people from fifty to sixty Assembly of God Churches in the State had brought their instruments. This 125-piece combined orchestra — if it could be called that — played for forty minutes before the evening service.

At such camp meetings, the orchestra was usually a disaster, for each person had his own favorite tempo for a given song, and some of the musicians would not budge an inch. I would try to pick out songs familiar to everyone and then make arrangements of what instruments would play which parts and established the tempo. I would choose the song, beat the tempo on the podium, and then go and lead the orchestra from the piano. The favorite was four-part harmony with all horns—really a beautiful sound that always brought a round of applause, as did my prelude, which usually began with solo instruments, followed by the whole orchestra playing a rousing verse and chorus of a lively gospel song.

I received tangible rewards for using my God-given talents to bless the ministry of those meetings. I had come to the camp meeting with only $10 and was very sparing in my cafeteria purchases. The hospitality chairman was the Reverend Gordon Lindsay, who later founded the nationally circulated *Christ for the Nations Magazine* and was the founder of "Christ for the Nations Institute" in Dallas, Texas.

Reverend Lindsay was at the cafeteria counter as I passed by, and he noticed my sparse dinner tray. He knew me because his wife, Freda, had lived near my family. He started questioning me about my money situation. Then he filled up my tray. When we got to the cash register, he filled out a meal card for me to cover my meals for the rest of the camp meeting.

He said, "This is the least that we can do for you. No one has ever been able to handle the orchestra as you have. Individual orchestra members usually go their own way, and, as a result, the music usually sounds terrible!"

This marked the beginning of my own ministry as a gospel musician and an evangelist in my own right. My skill as a pianist, song writer, and evangelist became known in ever widening circles throughout the West and, while still in my teens, I received a steady stream of invitations to conduct revival meetings, mostly in small churches.

As a gospel pianist (I called myself an "evangelistic pianist"), I was something of a rarity in those days. Many churches wanted their pianists simply to play four-part harmony as songs were written, but my improvisational playing included elements of rag time, blues, and popular music of the day. Today there are many college-trained musicians incorporating such improvisational styles, but that was not the case in the 1930s and '40s. This set me apart and enhanced my popularity, especially with Pentecostal and African-American congregations.

As I saw the Lord blessing my multi-faceted ministries, I experienced a sense of destiny and was eager to understand just what the Lord had in mind for me. Knowing I was called to full-time ministry, I determined to discover God's specific will for my life. This became the focus of my free time during the three-week camp where I served as pianist and music director for Evangelist Price. The whole three weeks I prayed after each service, and until or beyond midnight I enjoyed beautiful, rare and special moments in prayer followed by long waits. The last day came with still no answer from the Lord. Following the afternoon services I went to the prayer room as usual and knelt, not praying a word for about fifteen minutes, and then the Lord spoke one word, "Go."

"But, Lord, where shall I go?" I thanked the Lord for this word, but I wanted to know where.

When the Lord spoke to me, I recognized His voice immediately. There was no question in my mind that it was the Lord. People have often asked me, "Well, how do you know it is the Lord?" You just know. I would call the voice that I heard partially audible. It was one that I definitely heard with my ears as well as my other senses. It brought with it a sense of wonder and moments of awe afterwards. It was an answer to my three-week supplications of what the Lord wanted me to do with my life, and He said one word to me, "Go."

I began to search in the Bible for verses with the word *go*. A number from the Old Testament seemed not to be relevant to my situation, but then, as I turned to the New Testament, my eyes fell upon Matthew 10:6: "But go rather to the lost sheep of the house of Israel and as you go, preach, saying, The Kingdom of Heaven is at hand." This struck me as a confirmation, but, as I read verse 9, "provide neither gold nor silver, nor brass in your purses," I felt a fear that I had never felt before. To begin a journey toward an unknown destination without money in your pocket was unthinkable, even in Depression days. I suddenly felt hunger pangs and broke into a cold sweat. I found that the fear of hunger was as bad as hunger itself.

I had gotten a ride to camp from Portland in a friend's automobile and had come with only $10 in my pocket. I had made a comfortable bed for the warm summer nights under a tarpaulin, using the tall grass that had been cut and piled in stacks on the campground the week before the camp opened. No one had disturbed my belongings throughout the entire three weeks.

Four or five small gifts had been pressed into my hands during the first two weeks of the camp meeting, but no one had shaken my hand in this way during the last week. My cash resources were dwindling. Then someone gave me a crisp, new five-dollar bill on the day that an offering was being taken for a new campground and a new tabernacle.

While the service was in progress, the Lord spoke to me to give the largest bill I had—the five-dollar bill. With it I had planned to buy my bus ticket home. It was a difficult decision for me, as I had never given such a large sum of money before. The five-dollar bill burned in my hand. I wished the preacher would stop talking about the projected tabernacle and pass the baskets. When the offering was finally taken, I put the five-dollar bill in the basket as it passed by me. I watched the basket as it was taken to the front and set on top of the stack of baskets with my five-dollar bill in view.

Despite Dr. Price's eloquence, I didn't really hear anything he said. I was questioning myself. Was the voice I had heard really the Lord? I needed new clothes. Mine, which had been handed down from a cousin who had now gone to the Naval Academy, were old and worn. I breathed a sigh of relief when the brethren removed the offering baskets and the service came to a close.

After the service I lingered in the prayer room on my knees. The Lord had told me to "go." I counted the money in my pocket and found I had $1.76. I asked the Lord where I could go with only $1.76. Again came the single word "Go."

This time it was filled with love and understanding and filled me with confidence; so I answered, "All right, Lord, I'll go. I don't know where, but I'll go." With that, I arose from my knees. The battle was won. I had received my answer.

As I walked through the large double doors out of the tabernacle, I encountered a minister whom I knew. He turned to me and said, "I see the Lord has answered your prayer. Praise the Lord." To me there was nothing unusual other than my happy confident feeling. I didn't know why he said that to me. He later told a mutual friend that as I walked out of the tabernacle, my face shone as if I had seen an angel, but I was not conscious of the phenomenon.

I spent the last night in my makeshift shelter, then packed up my few belongings and made my way to the hospitality tent for breakfast. While I was at breakfast, the skies opened up with one huge thunderclap and the rain came down in torrents, the first significant rain since the camp meeting had started three weeks earlier. I thanked the Lord for keeping me dry, despite the fact that my shelter was not at all weatherproof.

The rain continued for awhile, but diminished to a drizzle and then gave way to sunshine as I reached the bus stop across the road from the campgrounds. About a dozen of us paid our 50-cent fare and boarded the bus for Salem, fifteen miles away.

Amid the happy chatter among the campers, my thoughts turned to my immediate future. The Lord had said, "Go," but had not said where or how. This matter of not knowing the immediate future is what concerns most people, and it concerned me, but now this was literally in God's hands. I didn't know what to expect. Soon the bus came to the last stop in Salem, on State Street. The time had come for me to prove my faith in God; to prove that He could lead and guide me, not only in my distant future, but also my immediate future.

While all of the other passengers headed south to another bus stop, I felt led to walk north. I stopped momentarily to recount the money in my pocket—$1.26. As I returned the money to my pocket, an elderly man in old worn clothes approached me and asked for a dime for a cup of coffee. It was my practice never to give money to panhandlers; however, if the person seemed deserving, I would take him to the nearest diner and buy him something to eat. I was tempted to turn away, but as I did, the Scripture came to me, "He that giveth a cup of cold water in my name shall not lose his reward." It was my first test.

A diner was on the corner, one of the original converted railroad dining cars, with tile floors and counters—a real beauty. I took him inside. He said quietly, "This boy is buying." I asked for coffee and a doughnut, the usual fare, but he pulled at my sleeve and pointed at a loaf of rye bread behind the counter. I nodded my head. The proprietor cut four thick slices and put butter pats on the plate and served him a cup of coffee. The man politely thanked me and said, "God bless you, young man." I put 25 cents on the counter and walked out. I now had just one dollar bill and a one-cent piece and, with God's instructions to "go," I walked north on State Street.

Walking on the east side of the street and about a mile from the edge of the city, I sensed the Lord telling me to cross the street. As I approached the opposite curb, I was impressed to look up. As I did so, I spotted a small sign for an upstairs mission above a ground-floor store on the corner. Had I been on the other side of the street, I would have missed it.

With my suitcase and bedroll, I climbed the stairs and discovered a simple chapel with a platform, pulpit, a piano, and benches that could seat about 100 persons. I called, "Hello," but nobody answered. After sitting to rest for a few moments, I went to the altar below the pulpit and knelt to pray. As I leaned against the altar bench, I felt the Lord give me the assurance that, so far, I was in His will. God had led me this way and He would continue to lead me.

After shouting another "hello" and receiving no response, I moved to the piano to practice one of the new choruses I had recently composed. As I played, unbeknown to me, a man and a woman appeared in the doorway at the back of the chapel and stood listening to me. After listening for some fifteen minutes, while I played some of my favorite choruses from the recent camp meeting, the man called out, "Brother Frey, welcome to Salem."

I looked up and recognized one of the ministers who had been on the camp meeting platform and his wife; the Reverend and Mrs. Fisher.

"The Lord has surely sent you, Brother Frey," Rev. Fisher said.

"Why did you say that?" I asked.

Rev. Fisher explained that a revival meeting was scheduled to start that night, and they needed an evangelist. However, everyone they had contacted was engaged elsewhere. When they had seen me at the camp meeting, both Mr. and Mrs. Fisher had been impressed to ask me, but were unable to find me because I had gone to the prayer room to pray. Meanwhile, they had to return home to conduct their own Sunday evening service. During that service they mentioned to the congregation their impression that I should be their revival speaker. Prayer was offered that they would find a way to contact me, which they had been unable to do despite calls to the campgrounds and to my home. By faith, the Fishers had announced on Sunday night that I would be there on Monday and now, here I was, sitting at their piano.

At their invitation, despite the fact that I was still only 17 years old, I quickly agreed to lead my first revival crusade and was so engaged for three weeks, singing, playing the piano, and preaching every night.

10
Exciting Revival Meetings

After that Salem revival, I felt impressed to go south. My next preaching assignment was at a large church in Oakland, California, which came about as a result of my contact with African-American pastors. This particular church had a white pastor, but half of the congregation was black. I preached at three services and then continued my journey south, still following the single-word command to "go," even though there were no preaching opportunities along the way.

When I arrived in Los Angeles, I made my way to the Angelus Temple, the giant headquarters church for the Four Square Gospel Church, built by the famous, flamboyant evangelist, Aimee Semple McPherson. I walked around the campus and sat in on a small service and then asked a student of the Bible school there if he knew of any "Holy Ghost rallies" being conducted in the city, as I would like to attend one. These were all-day meetings, which began at eight o'clock in the morning, lasted until midnight without a break and featured a different speaker every hour. They were the "rage" of southern California at that time. One was scheduled the next day at South Park Church.

I was the first person to arrive at the church the next morning. Shortly, about two-dozen people gathered in the cathedral-like auditorium, and the pastor in charge asked if anyone there could play the piano, as it would be a few minutes before the regular pianist would arrive. I did not respond at first, assuming that there was an abundance of competent pianists in that area. As I sat there, however, and the little congregation struggled through the first song unaccompanied, I was reminded of my agreement with the Lord as expressed in the old gospel song that came to my mind, "I'll go where you want me to go, dear Lord, I'll do what you want me to do." Besides, I never said, "No," to an opportunity. Another three dozen or so people had come into the auditorium during the first song.

"I feel led of the Lord to ask again. I know someone is here who can play the piano," the pastor said. "Would you please come forward?"

I raised my hand. I was installed at the piano and played the introduction for the called hymn and the choruses that followed, after which the pastor asked if I would stay at the piano for the day. I agreed to do so. Then the pastor said to the congregation, "The Lord has sent us a fine pianist." Before the day was over, a crusade was announced, I was asked to be the accompanist, and arrangements were made for me to stay in the home of a widow from the congregation.

That crusade lasted for three weeks, and then a Holy Ghost rally was announced for the 5,000-seat Angelus Temple. I was on hand early for the first service, claiming a good seat in the second row, having been informed that seats on the lower floor and in the balcony would fill up quickly. Sister McPherson was scheduled to speak at the 2:00 p.m. and 8:00 p.m. services.

About 11:30 the regular pianist left for lunch, and no one was at the piano when a chorus was called by a song leader. He turned around to the preachers on the platform, asking for a pianist, and the pastor of the South Park Church spotted me and motioned me to the piano. For the next two hours, I thoroughly enjoyed playing for this song leader, who was one of the finest I have ever played for. When the regular pianist returned to play for the 2:00 p.m. service, the song leader requested that I stay at the piano. If looks could kill, I would have been a dead man. There seemed to have been a feud between these two, and I had gotten myself in the middle of it.

Although Sister McPherson had her critics, I was thoroughly enthralled with her style of ministry. As a child, I had met her years before when she had come to my home church in Portland. What a speaker! Sister was dramatic, cultured, and poetic. A study of her sermons is a study of lyrical poetry set to an orchestra theme of Sebelius or Beethoven. She used her hoarse voice like a fine organ, with a master organist playing a fugue. It was sheer joy listening to her, even apart from the content of her sermons, which was always an inspiration. She preached the same Bible truths that thousands of ministers preached across the nation; but the difference was the unique way in which she presented them. When she swept onto the platform, she captivated even her staunchest critics.

It was during this October 1938, Angelus Temple meeting that I began what would become a common practice for me—the extemporaneous composition of songs and choruses in the middle of revival meetings. By the time I was given this unexpected opportunity to play for Sister McPherson, I had written a number of choruses, some of which were quite popular and were sung throughout the day at this crusade. My authorship of these choruses was mentioned during the services, and I suspected that I had been identified in this regard to Sister McPherson before she came to the platform.

Sister McPherson launched into her sermon on "The Blood of Jesus." At the end of her sermon she cried, "I know it was the blood! I know, I know, I know it was the blood for me!" I was sitting on the piano bench during her sermon, as I had been instructed. Sister said, pointing at me, with her flowing sleeves trailing behind the sweep of her arm, "This is good for a chorus, young man. Write one!"

From "Sister," a request was a command; but I was in a state of shock, surprised beyond measure. Then she continued with her sermon "I Know It Was the Blood."

On the platform was a most popular evangelist from southern California named Cyclone Jackson. He slipped out of his seat and came and sat beside me on the piano bench. I had taken out my pen, found a piece of paper and started to write the theme.

I know it was the blood. I continued to write
I know it was the blood. I know it was the blood for me

I could go no further. Cyclone Jackson asked what I had written, and I played it softly for him. He thought for a moment and wrote down these words: "One day I was lost." I was up on a high note and felt that I should stay there.

One day when I was lost.

We needed something to rhyme with "lost." Rev. Jackson and I put down several words, and finally we came upon the word *cross.* We both wrote, "He died upon the cross." Then I wrote the melody:

He died upon the cross.

The conclusion was automatic, for it was a line of resolve.

I know it was the blood for me.

Rev. Jackson and I sang and played it over softly, then called over the organist, Johnny Velerio, who caught the melody at first hearing. Then Cyclone Jackson went with my notes to the pulpit. (I was never able to retrieve them.) As he approached the pulpit, Sister said, "Well, let's have the chorus."

With the piano and organ accompanying Cyclone Jackson, we introduced my chorus written moments before in the packed Angelus Temple, which seated 5300 people. Then, led by Sister, the huge congregation sang the chorus many times, until my fingers were weary. She prayed for 1000 people to receive the infilling of the Holy Ghost and over 500 received the fullness that afternoon. Then she left the platform.

I was beat; tired almost beyond belief. I asked to be relieved. A new song leader took over, and the regular pianist rushed to the piano the moment I got up. She did not relinquish the instrument for the rest of the day, until requested to do so publicly by Sister McPherson so that I could come and play the chorus I had composed that afternoon.

The chorus spread like wildfire and became a standard all over America.

My reputation as a Christian songwriter spread and so did my popularity as a guest speaker and musician for revivals at churches throughout the West and Midwest. I was constantly on the go, ultimately ministering in 28 states. Many of the small churches at which I ministered experienced significant growth following my ministry there. Concurrently, my repertoire of original songs and choruses grew and spread from church to church around the United States and beyond.

11
Ministering In My Home State

The first indication of my unusual effectiveness with ministry to children came in a dying lumbering community called Beaver Creek, about 45 miles from Portland, Oregon. It was situated 10 miles from a main highway up a winding road that served a community six miles long. A generally poor community, it included one large farm, and a succession of small farms.

Mrs. Potter, the wife of the owner of the large 130-acre farm, had invited me there, apparently thinking I would never accept. She came often to Portland for special spiritual meetings and urged everyone she met in gospel work to come and hold meetings in the valley where she lived. Her invitation to me came after a fellowship meeting in a small eastside mission while we were having coffee and cake at the supervisor's home. After discussing the details of what would be involved in my going to that valley community, I told her I would have to pray about it. After doing so, I had a definite leading to accept her invitation and wrote her a letter instructing her to get permission from the trustees of the local church to hold a revival there.

Having no money for transportation and having heard nothing to indicate that the invitation was anything but valid, on the appointed day I prevailed upon my father to drive me to Beaver Creek, about 45 miles from Portland. A feeling of excitement began to grow within me as I anticipated this new adventure. In fact, I had butterflies in my stomach and a bit of stage fright as this was my first campaign within the State of Oregon. Following a pleasant drive, during which Pa expounded on the subject of sermonizing and commented on his favorite subject, St. Paul's writings on the old man and new man, we found ourselves at the end of the Potters' driveway.

"Would you like for me to accompany you to the house?" Pa asked me.

"No, thanks, I'd like to handle things myself" was my reply. I felt confident regarding my invitation, which seemed so explicit after Mrs. Potter and I had discussed it two or three times during her visits to Portland.

The driveway was a long one—about 300 yards. The day was warm—in the high 80's—as I walked with my large suitcase and a briefcase containing my Bible, concordance and loose-leaf sermon notebook. The white Victorian house was a large one for this community and was situated on an imposing incline, although the land was level where the house sat. The front porch was square with just enough room for a chair on either side of the ornately carved door. I rang the doorbell and waited for a while and then rang it again.

Soon a young boy opened the door, looked surprised to see me there and said, "Oh." I told him my name and said, "I think your mother is expecting me."

Without a word, he turned, leaving the door open, and disappeared through a hallway to the back of the house. I waited on the porch for more than a half hour before Mrs. Potter finally appeared. When she did she remarked, "I didn't think you would come! Come on in, but leave your bags outside. I must first talk to my husband. He doesn't know I invited anyone, and he doesn't like preachers!"

She also had not made any arrangements for the use of the church building, although she said she had been praying long and hard for a revival and was certain God wanted one in this Godless valley.

After a brief conversation, I went outside and sat on the lawn in the shade of a low tree waiting for her husband to come in from the fields. While I waited there for five hours, a multitude of thoughts and doubts ran through my mind: *How stupid I've been to have taken this woman seriously. If she were a real Christian, she would make me feel welcome instead of keeping me out here waiting with my bags on the porch. At least she could let the kids come out and talk to me.*

Eventually, the boy did come out and said, "I'm Bobby, and you're a preacher, right?" I replied that I was. After a brief friendly conversation, he said, "Daddy isn't going to like it. I don't think he's going to let you in the house." At that point his mother called him back into the house. As he started for the door, he said, "I gotta go, but I like you. I hope you can stay."

Still sitting on the lawn, I began to review the events of the afternoon and the nature of my thoughts and feelings. "Lord, forgive me for questioning Your wisdom," I prayed, "in bringing me here and please give me faith that I will find favor with Bobby's Dad. Then I took out my Bible and notebook paper and started writing some sermon notes. Just as I completed writing my first sermon for Beaver Creek, I saw the farmer come around the shady side of the house. I had lost track of time, but the length of the shadows and position of the sun told me it must be about seven o'clock.

Mr. Potter was very terse. "You're the preacher my son and wife told me about? You can stay." Then he turned on his heel and walked quickly toward the barn. As I stood watching him go, the front door opened. Mrs. Potter motioned for me to come in, but told me to leave my suitcase where it was. As I stepped inside, she delivered the "good news." Yes, I could stay, but no, I could not stay in the house. I could have my meals there, but not with the family. "I suppose you'll have to sleep in the barn."

Mrs. Potter was a wonderful cook and served me an excellent supper—some good food that had come from the farm and some of the nicer things that had come from the store in the town of St. Helens, about 12 miles away. As I ate, she filled me in on some of the details about the valley where she lived.

The valley was about eight miles long and two farms wide. It had been logged heavily some 40 years previously, and there were still loggers who made their homes there and traveled up the draws between the hills to where they were still cutting timber. It was said that more than a thousand people lived in and around the valley (I later calculated the actual population was about half of that).

After I finished eating, we retired to the living room where Mrs. Potter and I talked about the purpose of my coming. I asked if she had obtained the use of the closed church building and when we might begin meeting there. I had anticipated that we would begin holding meetings on the following day, which was Sunday. No, she had not seen the trustee about it. I would have to do that, but she had talked to the Sunday school superintendent, who had announced that Sunday school would be offered tomorrow morning. There had been no Sunday school there in over a year and no worship services in that building in four years. By phone, we exchanged essential information with the Sunday school superintendent and made plans for the next day. No future plans could be made until permission was obtained from the trustee.

Later, as I walked to the barn, I had to again suppress negative feelings that were rising within me. To be invited to someone's house and then be relegated to the barn was the height of indignity! On the other hand, I often had slept under the stars by choice and had slept on our lawn on hot summer nights; also, my family had gone camping often. This was not really all that bad.

By the time I reached the barn, I had gotten over my bitter feelings and was focused, instead, on my purpose for being there. I was there to win souls in a very needy valley. The church had been without a regular minister in forty years. The church building had been bought by the trustee and people of the valley. Regular services had been held for several years with the support of the Nazarene Church in town, which provided the ministers. The services stopped when an older man assumed the pastorate who was not interested in making the 24-mile round trip to hold Sunday afternoon services for a handful of people who would only pay him what it cost him for gasoline.

Inside the barn I climbed up to the hayloft where I created a comfortable bed by making a high pile of hay on which I spread my sheets and blankets. I was as comfortable there as I would have been in my own bed at home, the only significant difference being the hay and barn smells and the occasional piece of straw that blew across my face. Finally, I settled down to a solid night's rest, wondering what the morrow would bring.

12
Working With The Valley Folk

Early the next morning, I was awakened by the rattling of pails as Mr. Potter began milking his good herd of twenty Guernsey cows. Since it was so early, and I had been told what time I should show up for breakfast, I tried to return to sleep. I stayed in bed until I heard footsteps on the wooden floor beneath the hayloft.

Soon his son, Bobby, appeared on the stairs and said that I could wash and shave with hot water in the bathroom behind the kitchen. Then he said, rather firmly, "I don't like it that you're out here. I have asked Daddy and Mommy a hundred times if I could sleep in the barn, and they never would let me. Now, you come and this is where you are sleeping. Gee, it must be fun!"

I had gotten over my initial feelings of isolation and found that I could be quite comfortable in my hayloft room. I had found a stand where I could put my personal articles and had rigged up a rope on which to hang my clothes. I thought back to my boyhood when in fantasy play I would make a room underneath some huge blackberry bushes. This was not really bad.

It was only when I thought about the social implications of my situation that I still struggled a bit. I had not come on a youthful whim; the purpose of my visit had been urged upon me by the lady of the house on several different occasions with the assurance that I could stay in her guest room. I had had several similar invitations from different people in the past and had been able to distinguish between those who were merely making conversation and those who were sincere. Concerning this present situation, I had had no contrary feelings at all, only elation that at only 20 years of age I had an open door to minister in a valley where there was no active Christian ministry of any kind. The great question in my mind was, at my young age, could I do anything worthwhile among these farmers and loggers.

By the time I finished my preparations for the day, the family had finished their breakfast, and I took a seat at the table in the center of the large farm kitchen. Although it was a warm August day, there was a fire in the wood cook stove where Mrs. Potter prepared for me a large, delicious breakfast consisting of oatmeal mush, three eggs, fried potatoes, homemade bread with country butter, applesauce and coffee with heavy cream. I had hoped that Farmer Potter's truculence might have changed overnight, but Mrs. Potter informed me that her husband's attitude was still the same. Still, he had agreed to drive us to Sunday school in a little while.

Later, as I rode in the front seat of the family's year-old Chevy sedan—a symbol of Mr. Potter's prosperity and industry, nothing was said for the first mile or so. I attempted to break the ice with comments about the passing scenery, but they brought no response until we passed a recently cut hayfield.

"I have to cut my hay when the weather is dry," Mr. Potter said, then fell silent again.

I understood the importance of his comment, however. Western Oregon receives an excessive amount of rain, and August is usually the only dry month. Even then the weather can change suddenly and dramatically. If it rains while mowed hay is lying in the fields, a whole year's work can be ruined. Storing wet hay can lead to spontaneous combustion, and many a farmer has had his barn and cattle destroyed by fire because of trying to save hay harvested in the rain.

Nothing more was said the rest of the way to the church, which stood at the junction of three roads atop a small knoll. It was a plain unpainted building of typical size for a country church with seating for about 150 people. Outhouses were located at the rear of the church lot, and on top of a well near the front door of the church was an old-fashioned hand pump.

Word had gotten out about a young preacher coming, and some farmer, whose identity I never learned, had cut the tall grass around the building. I learned that there was some community interest in the building because it was also used for community meetings and as a polling place during elections.

Two cars were already in the parking lot and a few children were playing around outside. The interior of the church was plain but well built, and the walls were covered with unpainted wainscoting, which, while I appreciated its durability, struck me as drab and dingy. The meeting room was furnished with plain benches, a pulpit (the only stained piece of furniture in the place) and an old piano.

As we entered, the superintendent was working with some papers at a table on the side of the platform. She turned toward the door as we walked in, smiled, laid down her papers, and walked back to meet us. We shook hands in the middle of the center aisle. She impressed me immediately as a good woman and a beauty in her prime. Her suntanned skin and hands showed that she had been accustomed to outdoor work.

As we sat momentarily and talked over the plans for the morning, there was instant rapport between us, as there had been when we had talked on the phone the previous evening. I discovered that she had a real concern for the people of the valley and came to an understanding of her difficulties in ministering to them. She and Mrs. Potter were the only two "real" Christians in the area, but there was a great difference between them.

Mrs. Potter lived in the nicest house in the valley and was busy making a home for her hard-working husband and growing children. For her spiritual nourishment she would travel the 30 miles into Portland where she could stay with her sister and brother-in-law. She was always in the city for special services, which is where I had met her when I was preaching in the afternoon sessions of an all-day fellowship meeting.

Mrs. Foster, on the other hand, faced very different circumstances. Her husband was a logger and a drunkard. There were four small children in the home, which was set on 20 acres of marginal land on a hillside covered with raspberry and loganberry bushes. These and three cows kept the wolf from the door, but the Foster family's existence was a constant struggle.

Mrs. Foster explained that she had conducted the Sunday school for about eight years until a year ago. Most Sundays she had been alone with thirty unruly children and had finally closed the Sunday school because she felt it was inappropriate to have thirty uncontrollable children together without proper supervision. Still, she continued to subscribe to the *Sunday School Quarterly* and taught her own children at home.

At this point one of her small children piped up and said," But it's not the same as having Sunday school here."

This comment broke up the train of our conversation. Besides, children had begun running and playing around the benches. "See what I mean," Mrs. Foster said. Then, in a harsh voice, she yelled, "Sit down there! Stop running over there! Leave those song books alone!" She was trying to bring about a little order but to no avail.

One freckle-faced eight-year-old boy came up to me, looked close to my face and said, "Are you the new preacher?"

"Yes, I am," I replied, but he never had a chance to say any more to me because a sharp voice said, "Johnny, come over here and sit down!" He left me in a hurry.

About 30 children and five adults were assembled, although it took a little while to get the children seated and relatively still. Then Mrs. Foster opened the Sunday school exercises. While there was a piano, there was no pianist. The group sang a few choruses, but rather listlessly. It was a generally good, well-organized opening exercise; even though a year had gone by, most of the children remembered their part in it. All but one boy had even remembered to bring something to put into the offering (and he was reprimanded by the other boys for his failure).

After this Mrs. Foster introduced me. With a few words of self-introduction, I went to the piano and played a fast gospel song. The children suddenly came alive in a different way. Whistles, stomps on the floor, and shouts of "Play some more!" came forth spontaneously, to the surprise of all of us adults present.

Mrs. Foster was obviously nervous and tried to quiet the children, but I motioned to her that I had the situation well in hand. I acceded to their request and played another fast gospel song, after which came more whistles from older country boys and hollering from younger ones. As the room quieted down, the oldest boy present said, loudly, "Gee! When I came to Sunday school this morning I didn't expect to hear this. This is good!"

I taught them a few new choruses, including one with a little action to it. I decided against one with a lot of action, at least for now, because these kids were already active enough.

I had worked a lot with kids and had been successful in my own way. A few months previously I had left a little church in northwestern Washington, about 80 miles north of Seattle. When I had gone there, the Sunday school attendance had been 12 to 14, but when I left a year later, more than 70 were coming every Sunday. This success was not because of the organization or the literature or the teachers or the visual aids, it was solely accomplished from the platform by my use of certain methods to create interest, including action music and songs. Exercises are always a bore unless conducted with youthful imagination. A "dead" superintendent will create a dead Sunday school.

I had asked Mrs. Potter to give a short 10-minue lesson for the whole group after which I would close with a few words. She gave a very good lesson from the Book of John with a real gospel message. I had told the children to listen carefully because I was going to do something after she was through. I picked out words that she had used and deliberately made incomplete sentences. I had gotten through about four sentences when a hand went up, and one of the bright young boys exclaimed, "Mr. Frey, you left out a word!" He had caught on fast. I repeated the sentence and again his hand shot up. "You didn't say the word!"

I told him to keep the secret word until the rest of the children had it. By this time everybody wanted to know what the secret word was. I repeated the sentence again and then had each child come up and whisper to me what he or she thought the word was. Naturally, the adolescent boys and girls thought they had the right word, but only those who had been really listening to the lesson and my first remarks had it correctly. The bright boy and about 10 others got the correct answer. The rest had been cutting up too much to pay attention and thus failed to get it.

The word was *love*, taken from a rephrasing of John 3:16. We talked for a few minutes about God's love for mankind and the gift of His Son to redeem fallen man. Then we prayed, announced Sunday school for the following week and dismissed the children, who quickly disappeared out the door, leaving me with the five adults.

It seemed appropriate that we have a service, but we did not have permission to do so. The trustee was not present, and I was told, "He's backslidden and is back to drinking and smoking."

Along with four women, there was an old man present who said he had come just to be in a church building on the Lord's Day. He said he often walked two miles down one of the roads on Sunday morning and would sit on the church steps, praying that God would reopen the church doors.

"This morning was an answer to my prayer," he said.

He noted that he had been a lifelong Methodist, but had gotten far from the church and from God and was longing to return. Here in the woods, this was the only church available, and he hoped the church doors would be reopened on a permanent basis before he died.

We did have an adult Bible class and at about noon walked out of the building into a beautiful summer afternoon. Since Mr. Potter was not there yet to pick us up, Mrs. Potter, Bobby, and his sister, Grace, and I decided to walk with Mrs. Foster the short distance to her home. As we waited on the front porch of her unpainted, but otherwise nice, house, I learned a great deal about how hard her life was.

She was a woman of insight, gentleness and intelligence, but the cares of life had worn her down until she had become bitter about the events that surrounded her life. I tried to encourage her: "I came to help you in your work for the Lord. Don't give up even though it may be hard."

Just then, Mr. Potter's shiny automobile drove into the yard and seemed to contrast sharply with the poverty that surrounded us on the Fosters' property. As we got into the car, Mrs. Potter made a remark that let me know she was peeved at the fact that I was so supportive of Mrs. Foster. "After all, I'm the one who invited you here," she said. Not a very kind comment, to say the least.

13
Stepping In To Help

On the way home, as we rounded a curve, I saw a lane lined with cypress trees. Since timber is so abundant in Oregon, it is unusual to see plantings of shade trees. When you do see such plantings, it is usually because the owner of the land had come from Nebraska or the Dakotas and wanted to have familiar trees around them.

"Those are some trees," I remarked to Mr. Potter.

"Mr. Turner lives there," he replied. "He's a good farmer, but he has a lot of bad boys. Maybe you can do something with them. That's what you came here for, isn't it?"

Mrs. Potter hollered, "Henry!" and nothing more was said on the rest of the ride home.

As soon as the car stopped, Mrs. Potter indignantly got out and hustled Bobby and Grace into the house. Mr. Potter began fussing around with a car door latch, and I got the impression he wanted to talk. "Yes, I hope I can do something with the bad boys of the valley," I commented, "but I must know something about them. I'll need your help and the help of others who are concerned."

He told me about his problems with the Turner boys and about farming and his problem with maintaining his herd of cows. Some of the boys would run one of the cows out of the pasture into the road, shoot and butcher it and take the meat to town to sell it for whatever they could get for it. He said they had sold one of his milkers worth $300 for just $35.

The problem was that he could not prove anything, since the Turner boys had destroyed any evidence he would need. Of course, none of the Turner boys—from the oldest to the youngest—would admit anything. Their father became highly vocal and indignant at the accusation and terminated an arrangement they had where they shared farm equipment. As a result, Mr. Potter could not raise oats, which was a good crop for him, because he had no access to a combine. Mr. Turner had the only one in the county.

Again Mr. Potter said, "I hope you can do something with those Turner boys," then turned on his heels and stomped into the kitchen annex. I stood there for a moment trying to figure out his attitude. At least he was frank about his farming problems, but about nothing else.

I turned and walked toward the barn, took off my tie and coat and washed my hands and face at the spigot of the water trough alongside the barn fence. I got out a book of Spurgeon's sermons, took a chair I had found in the barn, leaned it against a tree and sat down for a long afternoon of pleasurable reading.

I did not expect to be called for dinner until after the family had finished eating, but after about an hour, Bobby came running toward me, almost breathlessly calling, "Daddy wants you to come and eat with us!"

As we walked toward the house, Bobby said, "After you were talking to Daddy out by the car, he came in and said to Mommy, 'The preacher isn't such a bad fellow after all.' Then, when we sat down to dinner, he said, 'Why don't we invite the preacher to eat with us?' So, Mommy sent me out to get you."

As we entered the kitchen, Grace and Mrs. Potter were preparing a place for me at the table. I shared a side of the table with Bobby, who smiled up at me with a look that told me I had a good friend in that big old house. The strained atmosphere was still there, but I tried to be a pleasant dinner guest. I guess I was trying too hard, because out of the blue Mr. Potter said, "Mr. Frey, I don't dislike you, I just don't like preachers!" and the atmosphere became even more intense.

When dinner was over, I went back to the chair against the tree by the barn and spent the remainder of the afternoon engrossed in the magnificent language of that eloquent Victorian-age British preacher.

As I considered my potential gospel work in the valley, I made arrangements with Mrs. Foster's drunken logger husband to take me to the trustee's home the following evening. I knew that nothing much could be done until I had talked with him.

In the morning Mr. Potter's greetings were less caustic when we encountered each other as he came and went from the barn and fields. However, when I asked him if there was something I could do to help him, he did not answer. Curiously, though, at suppertime he told me I could sit in the living room during the day if I wished. I replied that I would enjoy being able to do that in the morning and to read my favorite morning paper *The Oregonian*, to which they and many in the valley subscribed.

The day passed uneventfully, with me taking my meals separately from the family, Bobby helping his father in the fields and Grace helping her mother with the canning of fruits and vegetables for the coming winter. At seven in the evening Mr. Foster drove up to take me to the trustee's place. We drove to the extreme end of the valley, up a long steep gully and into an opening that overlooked the valley. The trustee's modern, natural wood house was set on the side of a hill, which struck me as an odd location, given all of the open land available.

The trustee greeted me in a friendly fashion and led me into a sparsely furnished living room. He told me that he had just given up on the church when the people did not respond and was glad if somebody else could do something. The church was ours to use as long as we preached the gospel and saved souls. A Nazarene by background, he seldom went to church anymore. He had no objection to the Full Gospel doctrine. "After all, if they live their doctrine," he acknowledged, "they are practicing their faith more than I am." He said he still loved God, read his Bible and, although he did smoke once in awhile, the rumors that he was drinking were entirely false. This information he volunteered without my questioning him.

He struck me as a mature person who would likely come and be a part of any successful gospel program going on at the valley church. If not, once a congregation was organized, it could elect a new trustee within a few months. We already had five adult participants, and that was a good beginning for even a brand new church in a deep Oregon valley.

After our formal meeting we stood on an open porch looking at the sunset and watching storm clouds forming beyond the valley to the south. The trustee was in a talkative mood; so, I listened.

"You will soon find out what it is that makes gospel work so difficult. There are two elements here: the good folks and the bad ones. There are over 130 children bused from this valley to the union school in Mt. St. Helens, 12 miles away. Some kids spend a lot of time on buses every day. There are the good children and the bad kids. The bad ones are real bad and have affected the little ones. I hope you can do something for these dirty little kids and those big bad boys."

I did not know about the big bad boys, but I was confident something could be done for the "dirty" little kids.

While we were talking, it began to drizzle; then there came one loud, unexpected thunder clap. I ran down the hill to the waiting car, and the clouds opened up just as I got in. Mr. Foster and I sat for about thirty minutes waiting for the cloudburst to subside before he drove slowly back to the Potters' farm. As we proceeded up the driveway, I could see the wagonload of hay in the barn. Mr. Potter had made it, and his second cutting of alfalfa hay was safely under cover.

I had been told that making arrangements for the additional use of the church building would be difficult, that the trustee had previously turned down two ministers who had wanted to use the building for similar purposes. I was not sure what had made the difference in my case, but I did discover later that he had been pleased when he heard about how well I had been received by the children the previous day. Although he had done little personally to influence the children of the valley, he was genuinely concerned for them and especially the influence of bad older boys on the younger children. He had instructed his own teenaged children to avoid all interaction with the Turner boys.

He said that the school buses were the problem. When the children had gone to school in the valley, they had been under the supervision of teachers who could control their behavior. However, now some children were riding a whole hour on the bus without strict supervision. The driver was too busy driving to handle any more than the most unruly behavior, and one driver never did anything at all in that regard, even though he was considered the best driver.

The school bus situation was on everybody's mind. Numerous community meetings already had been held concerning the matter. Despite some improvements, parents were still concerned. When I arrived back at the Potters' home, I asked Mrs. Potter if I could talk to her at length the next day concerning our plans.

"It would be nice if Mrs. Foster could be in on the conversation too," I added.

Mrs. Potter hesitated a bit and then said, "She won't come to my house even to visit. Could we go to her house and talk?"

I told her I did not think that was a good idea because we would be able to get very little done because of the screaming children. I was at an impasse. There was bitter feelings between the women, but I had hoped that my presence and the purpose for which I was there and their concern for children in the valley might overcome the tension between them. It appeared it would not be that easy.

Considering their feelings, I suggested we meet at the church. After a short phone conversation with Mrs. Foster, it was agreed that we would meet there after she had put her smaller children to bed the following evening. Mr. Potter would take us to the meeting, and Mr. Foster would drive us home afterward.

Predictably, much of our discussion the following evening focused on the "bus situation."

"At least the summertime gives us a rest, and we can undo the damage done during the school year," said Mrs. Foster.

Mrs. Potter said that she had made her two children sit together on the bus and that they never talked to the Turner boys, even on the farm. She was not, under any circumstances, going to let the bad children affect hers. They were going to act like a lady and a gentleman as long as she could control them.

Mrs. Foster expressed admiration for Mrs. Potter's determination concerning her children, but then said, "When you have a drunkard for a husband, who will discipline the children?" Mrs. Foster was too exhausted with farm chores to do much of that.

One of her boys had told her the whole story concerning the schoolhouse in the valley, which the bad boys had set on fire the previous fall. The act had been in retaliation for some discipline administered by the Union School in town against the older boys from the valley. They had planned it all in the back of the bus.

Word had gotten around that they were planning to burn the now unused schoolhouse, but nobody took the threat seriously until the whole valley was awakened by the blaring car horn on the trustee's car. He happened to be on his way home after a late diesel repair job up one of the draws. People from throughout the valley turned out to fight the fire. Bucket brigades were formed, but to no avail. Fire trucks arrived about an hour too late.

By the next morning nothing but a pile of smoldering ashes remained where the schoolhouse had been.

Who started it? Nobody knew for sure, but different ones were talking about it a few days before, and now the Turner boys had stopped talking. Angry and fearful eyes greeted them when they got on the bus the next school day, but months passed before the truth came to light.

One by one, the younger Turner boys turned on their eldest brother, who had done the deed "because no one else had the guts," he had said. He was suspended and eventually expelled from school and sent to a reform school. It was the solidarity of the children of the valley that had ultimately identified the culprit when school, town, and law enforcement officials could only point fingers of suspicion but accumulate little hard evidence.

I pointed out to the two mothers that the solidarity of the children was a good sign, but all they could see was the presence of the remaining Turner boys and their cronies living in the valley. They were seen as a constant threat.

"You'll see," they both warned me.

We made plans for the next few weeks. Revival services would be publicized by telephone by Mrs. Potter, Mrs. Foster, and two other ladies whom they would recruit. I began to plan for the next week and was busy for the next few days in my preparation for the meetings.

What would the ensuing weeks be like for me working among these farm people and their good and bad children? In some ways I was prepared, but in other ways I was not. Time would certainly tell....

14
Valley Daze

Sunday morning arrived, and Sunday school was more orderly and with a few more children in attendance. The evening service to me was a big question mark. Would the people come?

About 20 people actually did—this was a good start, and we had a good service. One twelve-year-old boy and an old man answered the altar call. The boy was sincere and said he wanted to be a good boy, but could Jesus help him and some of the bad boys in the valley. After the service Mrs. Foster took him to his home—a tar-paper shack on a knoll. I later learned that his father was another drunken logger.

The next day, Monday, was uneventful until the time of the evening service when Bobby told me to watch out for some of the boys who were talking about making trouble for me at church during that night's meeting.

As we opened the service, there was no one to be seen near the church except for those who were inside for the service. I was glad to see that the trustee was there. Attendance was about the same as Sunday night's and everything went smoothly until I sat down at the piano to begin the special musical portion of the service. As I struck the first chord, I was met with a great din of noise, which was not coming from the piano.

Immediately, I stopped playing, and the trustee jumped up and went outside, where he encountered several boys and a few girls rattling tin cans, banging old metal dishpans, pie plates, and empty oil cans. One boy had a big cow bell. I excused myself to the congregation and went outside. As

I passed to the door, some were saying, "See what I told you about those bad boys!"

The trustee and I stationed ourselves on opposite sides of the building so that we could intercept children as they ran from one side to the other. We managed to chase them away while stripping them of their noisemakers, which I threw inside the building through the open windows—it being a warm summer evening. After about a half hour, the trustee and I returned inside, and I continued the service, in spite of continual cat calls from some distance down the road.

The next evening was a disaster. Most of the adults had said they would not be back unless we could control the bad boys. The sheriff was not available to maintain peace around a country church. He was too busy dealing with an older breed of bad boys he was throwing in and out of jail on a variety of charges, including drunkenness, brawling and possession of stolen goods. The whole area was noted for such things. Was it any wonder the children followed a similar pattern?

There were only a few adults present, and outside the boys were hollering for their noise-makers. One boy's father came and scolded me for running after his son and scaring him. He then told me what the men up in the logging camps were talking about. They were going to burn down the church and maybe even Mr. Potter's barn. It seems they harbored resentment against the Potters and against me without any real cause.

I told him Mr. Potter's attitude was not much different from his own, as far as I could see, but he did have one thing in his favor—control over his children! I then scolded him for the extremely bad discipline he had over his bad-acting son.

Eventually he apologized and said, "I guess you're right, Preacher. You know we have been without a preacher up here for so long, lots of us don't know right from wrong anymore." Then he started in on his young son and his friends.

"If any of you boys come down here again and bother this here preacher, I'm going to whip you. Do you understand?"

His son was sitting in the man's old pickup truck and did not look at his father while he was being scolded. Instead, he looked at me with one of the oddest expressions I have ever seen on a boy's face. His eyes were wide and brimming with tears. It seemed like a look of extreme shock and great fear. As the man started the engine and began to drive down the road, the boy's eyes were fixed on me until the truck disappeared around a bend and up one of the draws.

We conducted the evening service as though the noisy boys were not outside. Still, they competed with me during my sermon, some of them mocking me with my own words. Clever boys they were. They threw stones in through the door so that they would roll up the floor, making more noise than just dropping them on the floor with a bang would have. It appeared as though they had had experience in the art of disturbing a meeting. I later discovered that there had hardly been a public meeting in the valley that had not been disrupted in the same way.

The following night was another warm evening, and the boys were out again. However, they made less noise, and it was less sustained. The audience consisted of only Mrs. Potter, Mrs. Foster and the old man.

Mr. Potter had refused to allow Bobby and Grace to attend such a "disgraceful display of bad manners." In fact, he was so disgusted that he said, "I would leave this valley if I could just get a good price for my farm, but I kinda doubt if that's going to happen." He further commented that somehow he would be able to get along with rough elements of the valley if his wife "didn't always come along with those ideas of improvement among people who didn't want to be improved." In fact, for the safety of the farm, he would even be willing to make peace with the Turner family, in spite of what had happened to his prize cow, but his wife would not hear of such a thing.

Wednesday night was the straw that "broke my back." Again the night was warm, the congregation was the same trio as the night before, and the bad boys were out in renewed strength with a new supply of tin cans, horns, and cow and sleigh bells. They started their harassment the moment we entered the church and continued it throughout the entire service.

I told the boys I would not chase them away anymore and that I could stand the noise just as long as they could keep it up, (which, I must admit, was probably not entirely true). The din was most disconcerting, and I am certain that those present heard very little of what I said. Our songs were sung only to ourselves and to the Lord. At the end we had a prayer meeting. As we gathered in a tight little circle so we could hear each other, the noise abated and a boy looked in the back door.

A voice from outside asked, "What are they doing?"

The boy at the door responded, "I don't know."

"Are they just talking?"

"No, they have their heads bowed."

"Then they're praying. Come on, they're having a prayer meeting!"

For the next fifteen minutes we could hardly hear ourselves think, much less pray, but pray we did. In the process, the Lord gave me an inspiration. If the boys are like this during the evenings, what are they like during the day? Where do they gather? What do they do?

On the way home I remarked to Mrs. Potter and Mrs. Foster: "All the kids are doing is making noise. Not one thing has been touched. The church hasn't been harmed. Not one window has been broken. It's all just noise. That's all it is, just a lot of noise! If we try long enough and hard enough, there will come an end to that. "

I realized that I had to get acquainted with these boys, but where? Not at their homes. I would have about as much chance of making progress at some of their homes as snow in July. I was sure that I would not get a word out of them and that their parents would resent my presence.

I discovered that all the kids in the valley gathered for swimming behind the house of the Smith family, whose boys were among the nightly noisemakers. A small, shallow creek ran the length of the valley and formed a small pond behind the Smith's house. I had not thought about swimming since coming to the valley and had left my swimsuit in Portland. When I started to talk about the popular swimming hole, Mrs. Foster told me that she would not let her children swim there because she did not believe in mixed bathing.

The next day was very hot, and about mid-afternoon I started walking toward the Smiths' house. It was a pleasant three-mile walk along the dusty country road. Few cars passed by, and along the way I got acquainted with two elderly couples who had heard the noise at the little church. Both expressed their dismay at the trouble in the valley, but promised to be in church Sunday morning, although one was Catholic ("Any church is better than none," they said) and the other was Methodist. Both were far from their churches in both distance and practice.

About a half mile from the pond I could hear the children playing. They spotted me from about that distance.

"Here comes the preacher!" someone cried, and several boys rushed up to me.

"We don't want you here. Don't bother our fun," they told me.

I had them in a fix. It was so beastly hot that everyone wanted to swim, and they did not know how to stop me from being there. They knew better than to use physical force. They knew the local police would not hesitate to arrest them and charge them with assault and battery.

The oldest and biggest boy (only a couple of years younger than I) came up to me and said, "Preacher. I'll throw you out if you don't get the heck out of here!"

I replied, "The only one who can throw me out is the woman who owns this place. I'll talk to Mrs. Smith."

Mrs. Smith was standing on the back porch of a dilapidated, unpainted house. As I walked up to her, she said, "I know who you are, Reverend Frey. You can stay. I hope you can calm these kids down. Nobody else can do any good with them."

Then, in a hard, gruff voice, she said to the boy who was challenging me, "And you leave the preacher alone or I'll throw you out of here! And I can do it!" She did not look that strong, but she said it with such force that, to the obvious amazement of the 40 other children looking on, she cowed the boy who was almost twice her size and would have been quite capable of beating me in any physical contest.

As I sat down by the edge of the creek and looked over those gathered there, I recognized some who had been to Sunday school and some who had been among the noise-makers. For the longest time, they stood or sat motionless, looking at me. It seemed like a movie scene stopped in mid-flight.

I was intruding. I knew it. I did not belong there, but I was after something; I knew not what. The inspiration I had was to get acquainted with the kids in their own fields of play.

I spotted a Sunday school girl and called out to her by name. "Don't let me stop you from swimming, Ginny. Not on a hot day like this. Go ahead and swim, kids. Don't let me spoil your fun."

They took another look at me. Some smiled, and then one of the boys who had been a cowbell ringer dove into the water. They were off, making as much noise as they had before my intrusion.

Presently, the cowbell ringer came out of the water and sat down beside me. "You're a funny preacher, coming to watch us kids swim," he said. "Do you like kids? Do you swim?"

"Yes, I love kids and I love the water, but I came here to preach and didn't bring a swimsuit because I didn't think I'd have the opportunity to use it."

At this, he jumped up and ran into the water, hollering, "Hey, kids! The preacher likes the water," and then he dove in. When he surfaced, he yelled, "Hey, Preacher, why don't you come in? The water's good!"

At that point other children came up and sat beside me and began making small talk. One girl said to me, "I'm a good girl, and will have nothing to do with those terrible bad boys. Did you ever see such bad boys in all your life?"

I replied that they were pretty bad, but I hoped that they would be better before I left.

"Not these boys," she said. "They're too bad. Even the kids in Mt. St. Helens won't have anything to do with kids from the valley because of them. I hate them!" she said vehemently and then started walking toward her home.

With some urging, I persuaded her to stay until I left. Then I took off my shoes and socks and waded with my pant legs pulled up to my calves. This obviously pleased many of the children. Shortly, I dried my feet, put my socks and shoes back on, and started to leave.

As I left, I got a mixed reaction ranging from "Good bye, Reverend Frey. Will you come back tomorrow?" to "Good bye Preacher, I'll see you at church tonight — outside!"

One boy said, "Don't come back here. Leave us alone. We can't have any fun while you're here."

Another child said, "Come back tomorrow. I like it when you're here. The boys behave better." I also received a word of thanks from Mrs. Smith as I walked down the road in the company of about a dozen children.

I was not sure what my visit to the swimming hole had accomplished, but at least the worst of the noise-makers were talking to me. At the church they would listen to nothing I said.

As the time for the evening service arrived, so did the boys, outside as expected; however, they had lost their fire. By the end of the service—attended by a few more people, it was actually quiet. The 20 boys who had gathered there earlier were nowhere to be seen as we left the church.

When Mrs. Potter discovered where I had been that afternoon (she only knew I had gone for a walk), she expressed her disapproval. If I had gone swimming where there was mixed bathing, she would not come to hear me preach anymore.

I explained to her my feelings concerning the subject and that my sole purpose was to reach the bad boys of the valley and that I needed to search for ways and means for doing that. "I believe this is what the Lord has shown me to do," I explained. I didn't have a bathing suit with me, but if I felt it would break down this wall of rebellion, I would go swimming with all my clothes on.

That seemed to placate her. It was acceptable because I had not been in a bathing suit where the girls were. Such were her puritanical ideas. Poor Bobby and Grace were sweltering in the heat and would have loved to have gone swimming. They said nothing, but I could see it in their eyes.

At about mid-afternoon on the following day, I again made my way to the pool. When I got there I was greeted with a variety of cat calls, whistles, and cheers and more friendly greetings. After a while the bell-ringing boy dared me to go in the water. I had purposely put on my oldest pants and shirt and was prepared for such a challenge. All the boys began chanting for me to get in the water and kept it up for a long time until the girls began chiding the boys for harassing me.

"He'll come in when he gets good and ready!" one of the girls said, and then I started in. This time there were no cat calls or Bronx cheers; only whistles and screams. I was in with my pants rolled up above my knees. The rest of the afternoon was just plain unadulterated fun for me and for the kids. Later, one of the boys commented, "I have never had so much fun in all my life!"

When I walked out of the water, I knew things would be different. My clothes dried out in a short while, and I walked back to the Potters' farm with half of the children following me. As they reached the lanes leading to their various farmhouses, each came to me to say how much fun they had that afternoon. Several girls thanked me, telling me that it was the first time the boys had behaved themselves.

That night was different indeed. The same boys showed up, but there were no bells or cans in their hands. They just stood outside the open windows and talked or listened. Soon the bell-ringer stood briefly in the doorway, then came and sat down. Later, others followed him. Soon, the two back rows were filled with my noise-making crowd, only this time they were as quiet as a group of boys can humanly be.

After the service, I walked back to talk to the boys, but before I could get to them, all had left except the bell-ringer, who stayed to apologize for his bad manners.

15

The Valley Is Changing

Although the valley was challenging, eventually the revival gained momentum. Loggers in their rough logging clothing were coming down the draws with their families for the evening services.

We sang songs like *"The Old Rugged Cross"* and *"What a Friend We Have in Jesus,"* and everybody loved them. Some were getting truly converted. Sunday night every seat was filled. Virtually every family but one from the valley and surrounding draws were coming.

I could see a change in the way children played during the afternoon swim at the Smith Pond, but I had made not one bit of progress in reaching the Turner boys and their father. The Turner boys never set foot on the church grounds at any time, even during the first period of noise making, although it had been their suggestion to harass the preacher that had started the whole thing off.

The two younger Turner boys were civil enough. I met them during the afternoon swim. Even though they had a reputation among the kids of the valley for being really tough, I could not see that they were much different from other kids. They were actually better off than most in the valley, as their father was a hard-working and successful farmer. Money or the lack of it was not their problem.

The real root of the problem was their lack of a mother in the home. She had abandoned her family while they were still very young. It had happened after a drinking party at which several couples exchanged their mates for a night. The fact that this was public knowledge, even among the children, did not help the Turner boys. Most of the fights they got into resulted from real or imagined insults concerning their mother, whom they seldom saw and hardly knew.

I had wanted desperately to talk to the Turner boys and made several attempts. Nine-year-old Tom, the youngest, was the only one with whom I actually became acquainted. That started the first two times I went to the Smith Pond. Once Mr. Turner found out about my being there, he made Tom go swimming in the morning when I was not there.

I prayed much about it. In fact, I prayed through one whole night and did not fall asleep until after Mr. Potter had started milking his cows in the morning. I was getting anxious. After all, I had spent three weeks in the valley and not one Turner had come around even to look at me.

For all they may have done to earn a bad reputation, I still found something admirable about the Turner boys — they could and would work the fields like men. That was still the era of horses on the farm. Limited mechanization had come, but with only one tractor on a farm, horses were employed when there was more than one field to be plowed.

I saw nine-year-old Tom handle a team as though he had done it for many years. One day, I sat on a fence admiring the way he managed the horses and the mowing machine. When he saw me there, he stopped his horses and stood near me. I opened the conversation by asking him the names of the horses. He proved to be a bright, intelligent boy and a little large for his age.

Coming right to the point, he commented, "Preacher, I'd like to come to church someday, but my daddy won't let me."

"Why not?" I asked

"Well, he says religion is a lot of humbug and the churches are full of hypocrites."

"What do you believe?"

81

"Well, I don't know what I believe, but I know what I feel. When someone talks bad about God and the little church, I feel bad inside. So, I know they're wrong or I wouldn't feel that way. What do you do in church, Reverend Frey?"

I told him we sing songs for boys and girls and older people, preach and pray to God.

"Did you ever pray, Tom?" I asked him.

"Yes, I did, Reverend Frey. When all the boys went to make all that noise outside the church, I felt real bad inside and I went to the woods and asked God to show me Himself so I could tell Daddy there was a God. I waited a long time. I didn't see anything but I felt really good inside. So, I don't care what Daddy says about God. I know He's there somewhere and that He listened to me talk. My older brothers are making fun of me now, but I really don't care because I feel real good when I think about God."

I asked Tom if he had a Bible, and he said his father would not permit one in the house. So, we made a plan. Tom revealed that Bobby Potter was already meeting secretly with him (something Mr. Potter knew about, but not Mrs. Potter). I would give Bobby a Bible, and he would give it to Tom, who would hide it under a corn crib near where they were meeting afternoons. At the end of my conversation with Tom, he got back on the seat of the mowing machine, gave a gentle snap of the reins and continued his cutting of the field of alfalfa hay.

This was my first knowledge of Bobby's meeting with the Turner boys—something I had suspected, but could get no admission from Bobby. No wonder he had always known what plans were cooking on the other side of the road.

When I told Bobby of the plans, he first smiled that big boyish smile of his and then froze. "You're not going to tell Mother, are you? She hates Tom and his brothers."

"No, of course not; this is just between you and Tom."

I felt a release to leave the valley now. Before the revival was over, approximately one-third of the children and adults in the valley had been converted. I was grateful for the way God had worked, in spite of what had seemed like incredible obstacles to my ministry; but I must admit I was looking forward to getting back home to my parents' house in Portland.

16
A Vision Of Things To Come

Following a revival, I would usually return to my parents' home to rest up and prepare for the next series of meetings. It was during one such respite, following an exceptionally effective revival, that I received a dramatic vision of what was to be the primary ministry of my adult life—ministering to children in New York City.

I experienced that vision in 1939, at the age of 21. I had just closed an outstanding three-week evangelistic meeting in Colville, Washington—population 3,000—which ultimately resulted in the growth of the sponsoring church from 250 to 1,000 members.

After spending some time talking with my mother on the morning following that revival, I was feeling very tired and returned to my bedroom. Looking out my bedroom window toward Mt. St. Helens, I prayed, asking the Lord for direction for my life. I offered myself to be a pastor, an evangelist, or a missionary, wherever the Lord would direct. Then I lay down and slept for several hours. It was as I awoke that the vision unfolded before me.

I saw the City of New York as one might from a helicopter. It appeared to me as though I was flying down the East River and up the Hudson River, over the tops of skyscrapers in Manhattan, and I landed on the corner of 63rd and Central Park West.

As the vision continued, I traveled through the city, following the parkways and over a church in Brooklyn. Eventually, I saw a very dilapidated building on the Lower East Side of Manhattan that needed new plumbing, wiring, and a complete overhaul. I recognized that the building had special significance within the vision. On the surrounding streets, I observed dirty little children playing among broken-down automobiles.

As the vision gradually ended, I knew in my heart that it represented God's call on my life. As sure as I was of that, however, it would be 15 years before I would actively pursue that vision. I was very close to my mother and longed to tell her about the vision, but I refrained from doing it because I believed it would break her heart to think of me moving to the East Coast, so far away from her. I did not tell her for two years. I did tell a friend about my call, but the friend merely scoffed, laughed and ridiculed me. Much time would pass before I would speak of the call again.

In the intervening years, I continued active in ministry. I conducted evangelistic meetings in 28 states, and, for eight years, I pastored Everybody's Tabernacle, the largest interdenominational church in Detroit, Michigan.

In 1950, I made my first journey to New York City in an attempt to confirm the vision I had received a decade earlier. Arriving in New York on the coldest day of the year, I checked in to the Millner Hotel on 29th Street and Broadway. My objective was to read the pulse of the big City and get a sense of where to start a ministry. I spent several days handing out gospel tracts to unfriendly passersby, some of whom cursed me and even spit at me. After six bewildering months, during which I felt direct satanic oppression, I boarded a westward train to return to Oregon. As the train passed through Philadelphia, I felt something I had never felt before. The demonic power began to lift from my body by degrees as the train proceeded west. By the time the train passed Lancaster, PA, my body felt light and free again.

Back in Portland, Oregon, I began attending Wings of Healing Church, whose pastor was my friend, Dr. Thomas

Wyatt. When Dr. Wyatt asked me how I liked New York City, I responded firmly, "I'll never go back to New York City as long as I live!"

Dr. Wyatt then invited me to join his staff and work with the church's choir. I could not have been happier. Music had been such an essential part of my life and ministry.

For four years, I had served as musical director of the Wings of Healing radio broadcast, which aired on about 90 stations. God's special blessing was on my music ministry, and it was during this time that I wrote some of my best-known choruses, including "I've Got Peace Like A River," "This Is My Commandment," "This Is the Day," "He Is Lord," and "Isn't He Wonderful."

Eventually, I all but forgot about my earlier calling to New York City and was settling comfortably into life in Portland, seeing the Lord blessing my music ministry and moving in marvelous ways. I was on the verge of accepting an offer from my father (a builder) to build me a home in the Portland area and was negotiating with the owner about a piece of property overlooking the Columbia River Gorge in Troutdale, near Portland. The owner agreed to sell me a five-acre parcel, and a date was set for us to meet to close the deal.

Then, I fell deathly ill. Bed-ridden, I was examined by my cousin, a physician, who declared he could find nothing wrong with me and said that I could get out of bed. However, I was so weak that I could walk only short distances.

During this time of convalescence, I read a book titled *Forty Years in China*, written by a missionary named Baker. The book reminded me of my neglected call to New York City and helped to bring me under such conviction that waking from a dream one day, I said, "All right, Lord, I'll go back to New York City, even if I have to walk across the American continent." And I meant it.

I felt better immediately and began writing to pastors to set up meetings and crusades across the country. One Thursday, during a visit to downtown Portland, I experienced a unique sight or vision.

As I walked along 42nd Street toward the bus stop, to my left, on the east side of the street, I noticed a 20-acre parcel of vacant land. Then, I witnessed a mirage that made the snowfields of gorgeous Mount Hood appear to touch that parcel of land, although the mountain was fifty miles away. Beyond the mirage I actually "saw" the skyline of New York City, and I again vowed to the Lord that I would go to New York, even if I had to walk.

Upon returning home, I found a letter in my mailbox from a Medford, Oregon pastor; it said, "Brother Frey, we'll have a revival for you starting Sunday." The pastor said that the Lord had awakened him at three o'clock in the morning and had told him to write to me and set up the revival.

The ensuing year was my busiest ever, in terms of meetings, with hardly time to get from one meeting to another as I headed across America. Still, in the back of my mind was the vision God had placed upon my heart and mind, which was only getting stronger.

17
Surprises In New York City

I arrived in New York City on August 1, 1954, the hottest day of the year.

Encouraged by some New York pastors I had known from the past, I preached in various churches in the New York area, but refrained from holding revival meetings while I sought to establish the ministry for which I knew God had called me.

As I settled into life in the big City, I needed to find a job to sustain myself. First, I sold haberdashery and then house wares. On weekends and after work, I would ride subway trains and buses looking for the building that God had showed me in that original vision. After some weeks, I found a building at 9-2nd Avenue that seemed to fit most closely with the one in the vision.

It was relatively soon after my arrival in New York that Helen Parsons and I met and began a dating relationship. Helen adds her reminiscences of this special time when God brought two unlikely people together to forge a strong marriage that would bless many people over the years.

* * * * * *

Since early childhood, I had developed a great respect and admiration for my Aunt Mildred Paine, my mother's younger sister. She was a missionary to Japan and when she came to the United States on furlough she would spend several weeks at our home, helping mother around the house, and spending quality time with us five children. As she told stories about the children at Ai Kei Gakuen, (Garden of Love), in Tokyo, I was impressed, and felt in early teen years that God could use me in Japan, following in Aunt Mildred's footsteps. After two years at Providence Bible Institute, I was informed that I would need to complete college before applying as a missionary to Japan. In 1949, I attended Roberts Wesleyan College in N. Chili, N.Y., graduating in 1951 with a B.A. degree. I met the Methodist Board of Foreign Missions at the headquarters office in New York two weeks prior to graduation and was accepted as a missionary to Japan after successful completion of some requirements. In 1954, I went to New York focused on the goal ahead. I got a room at an international house owned by the Methodist Church in Greenwich Village, within walking distance from the Methodist headquarters office at Fifth Avenue and 20th Street.

Out strolling one Sunday evening, I was attracted by the spirited sounds of piano music flowing out from a church building bearing the name "All Peoples Church." Inside, I was greeted with a warm welcome by Pastor John and Mrs. Derr, who were former missionaries in India. There was a wonderful presence of the Holy Spirit, and my heart was warmed by the love and kindness of folks there. God was clearly ministering in the services and I was drawn closer to Him in ensuing days and weeks. One Sunday evening as I was playing the piano for the service, a tall, handsome young man slipped into the service. After the service I was introduced to Marvin Frey, who, it turned out, was a fellow occupant of the large apartment building in which the Pastor lived. That introduction marked the beginning of a major alteration in the direction of my life. A quickly developing friendship soon progressed to courtship, and before long I found myself informing the Methodist Missionary Board that God had changed my plans for missionary (or ministry).

As we dated during the very hot summer—going to beaches and parks, trying to cool off—Marvin and I shared the deep feeling that God in His love and grace had brought us together. Years before me met, we each dedicated our lives to God, to go wherever He might call us. As Marvin obeyed God's call to move from the west coast to minister to children on the streets of New York City, God miraculously joined our hearts and our vision together.

By the time Marvin met me, he had written an amazing repertoire of songs, many of which were becoming standards among Christian congregations of virtually every denomination. Sometimes on dates, Marvin would bring a large notebook of his original music. He enjoyed singing these joy-filled songs, as I listened and felt it a privilege to have a private audience with the composer of songs like "Kum Ba Yah," "Do Lord," "I Know It Was The Blood." "I Have Decided To Follow Jesus," and many others.

* * * * * *

One evening as we were walking down Bank Street in Greenwich Village, I told Helen that I had just lost my job at a housewares store, but that I would find another one. Then I asked her if she would marry me. Without hesitation she answered, "Yes."

Soon I found another job as assistant manager of a housewares store in Woodside, Queens that had a six-person sales force. Among my responsibilities were the ordering, stocking and delivery of merchandise. Because the store dealt in high-ticket items the job required a very responsible person who could protect the store against losses through theft.

When I told my employer that I would be getting married two days after Christmas, he objected strongly. So, when I left to get married, my boss promoted one of the salesmen to the assistant manager position with the intention of dismissing me upon my return. This highly questionable decision was thwarted, however, when the newly appointed assistant manager displeased with the job, quit after two days. When I returned to work, my job as assistant manager was resumed.

We were married on December 27, 1955, in the West Barre Methodist Church where Helen grew up. It was a lovely wedding with the blessing of friends and family from near and far. Helen's only sister, Esther Huestis, missionary in Brazil (with her husband, George), was matron of honor. Close friend and professor at Roberts Wesleyan College, Dr. Stanley Magill performed the ceremony with other pastors assisting. Rev. Vernon Thompson, my brother-in-law from Ohio was best man, and my long-time friend and pastor in Brooklyn, Rev. Clair Hutchins blest the ceremony with his rich tenor voice.

One day while making deliveries across Northern Boulevard in Jackson Heights, Queens, I saw a huge plot of ground which I discovered was the sight of the original LaGuardia Airport. During World War II it had been occupied by wartime housing, which had since been demolished. Now it was being sold off to developers. I recognized that with its wide-open space, accessibility to subways and major highways, this would make a great site for a major tent crusade. Although I realized that locating the owner could be a major challenge, I stepped out on faith to acquire it for that purpose.

While Helen continued her full-time job at the Methodist headquarters offices, we both agreed in faith that I quit my job in order to devote my time to the tedious task of locating the owner. The rigorous legal process took two months of diligent hard work, sorting through many deeds before the owner's name finally surfaced. When contact was made, I found that he occupied an entire floor of New York's Pierre Hotel. His first question was, "How did you find me?"

When I presented my proposal to the owner, he was agreeable. I then contacted several pastors, informing them that a parcel of ground had been located within the City that would be large enough for a crusade tent. As I committed the matter to God, I told Him, "if You want a revival in New York City, You, Lord will have to bring it in Your own way." Then I let it rest.

Subsequently, while I was in Massachusetts conducting a revival meeting, a knock came on my door at three o'clock one morning. It was my host pastor saying that Evangelist Jack Coe was on the phone. Brother Coe told me that he had heard through Oral Roberts that there was a plot of ground in Queens appropriate for a major tent.

One weekend shortly thereafter, Helen and I traveled to Washington, D.C. to meet with Brother Coe and his business manager. Plans for a revival were formulated, and in October 1956, what was described as the world's largest tent was hauled from Dallas, Texas to Queens, New York. Churches throughout the New York City area began prayer vigils for the tent crusade. I had been praying since coming to the City for a break-through of God's Holy Spirit that would turn people's hearts to God. It was a blessing to be actively involved in the organization of the crusade, and to supervise the large number of ushers. Meetings continued with Brother Coe preaching almost nightly for six weeks, to a combined total attendance of over 25,000. The impact on New York City, the five Burroughs, and up to fifty miles in every direction was truly awesome and long-lasting. Thousands of individuals accepted Jesus Christ as their Savior, and as a result, many new churches sprang up, and existing churches were miraculously revived. Only a few weeks after the crusade closed, Brother Coe had returned to his home in Texas and was suddenly taken home to heaven with a heart attack. His passionate love for God and the souls of men has left a powerful witness to countless thousands of people.

18
The Challenges Of Starting
A Children's Ministry

After our marriage in 1955, we rented an apartment on the fourth floor of a ten-family apartment house on West 94th Street. It was once a German community, but when we moved there it was a mixed neighborhood, comparatively quiet except for noisy Columbus Avenue. We had a pleasant three and one-half room apartment in the back. The building was on a court, with six large windows facing the court and one window in the back. The apartment was so situated that we always had a nice breeze, which was good except for one thing. Everything would be covered with layers of grimy soot and grit. Keeping an apartment clean in Manhattan can be a back-breaking job. I personally would give up and let a few layers collect before tackling the cleaning job, but not Helen. She tackled every layer as it fell on our floors and furniture.

The block we lived on began to deteriorate after it was identified as an urban renewal area and was slated for demolition. Responsible people would not take a lease and landlords filled the apartments with the worst kind of tenants. Across the street were winos, prostitutes, and drug addicts. On Columbus Avenue the railroad flats that ran front and back began to be filled with Puerto Ricans who lived normal, decent lives but were often noisy. What a change it must have been from the quiet old Germans who occupied the block before we moved in. Our court windows faced the back window of the railroad flats on the Avenue. During the summer months, Latin folks lived on the back fire escapes. Day and night you heard bongo drums, blaring radios, hi-fis with speakers out the window going full blast, and noisy children and women screaming in Spanish, trying to be heard above the other noise.

We tolerated the noise, but when personal safety became a concern, that was another matter. We decided we had to move for our own protection. The drug addicts across the street made living there too dangerous. Helen had to take a taxi to work, and coming home after dark she could be accosted between the cab at the curb and the apartment house door. One evening after returning home from a tent crusade, someone broke in and stole something special to Helen, the wrist watch given her by her family for graduation from college.

After four years we moved to a nicer apartment in Riverdale, Bronx. The rent was double for the same three and one-half rooms, but now Helen would be safe. We had a beautiful view of the Hudson River. It was a quiet Jewish, middle class neighborhood and we enjoyed the comfortable surroundings.

While living on 94th Street we attempted to make contacts with the children on our block, but with no success. How does one begin a children's work on city blocks? The best way I discovered is to let the children do it. One child leads to another and soon you can reach a whole block. We began to sort out our thoughts concerning our work; of what sort it would be, to whom, and for whom it would be. Blunt, frank and harsh speech will instantly repel teenagers; they know all about it. Children and teens respond to love, understanding and kindness. We needed to devise a more gentle approach in working with these poor children. It was not our purpose or calling to clean up the discarded lives, but to mold the children's lives when they can best be molded, while they are young.

However, New York City kids are smart. They know when someone is trying to shape them, influence them, or direct them, and they will frankly tell you so. They will make up their own minds. We could only love them in everything, and teach them what they don't know. They have curious minds and desire knowledge. They understand love, while at the same time seeking acceptance. It is on these principles that we have based our ministry among them.

I tried to read everything that had been written about children's ministry in New York City, but very little was published regarding the sub-teenage level. Several fine volumes have been written about the drug problems among teenagers. There is that wonderful witness to Christ's saving power, "The Cross and The Switchblade," by Dave Wilkerson.

When we started our Sunday school in the rented facilities of a Hungarian Reformed Church, I wondered how we would make contact with children. I had seen many children on the street, but in this neighborhood you could not approach the children on the street unless they first approached you. If you did, you would get a cold eye of suspicion and then a look of amusement or a cold glare with the response of "Get lost!" virtually ending any possibility of working with the children in that block.

These children were confronted by all sorts of do-gooders and had become calloused toward anyone introducing religion— at least on the immediate surface. However, children of the street have an insatiable curiosity. So, if you do anything different, new or unfamiliar, whether good or bad, you will soon draw a crowd of children around you.

One day, I was standing on the church steps when a pretty 10-year-old girl walked up to me and asked, "Are you the new preacher?" I told her I was holding services in the building and hoped soon to start a Sunday school. She told me that her father was Baptist and that her mother was Russian Orthodox and went to church. Her grandfather had been a Baptist preacher at a church around the corner.

She had gone to a Sunday school before, but had stopped because that church taught that only their members were true Christians: she knew that some of her friends who went to different churches were Christians, too. I was surprised to hear this from a 10-year old.

Then she asked me, "Do all the children have to join your church to go to your Sunday school?"

I replied, "No, you don't have to join our church at any time, and if we begin a Sunday school, it will be open to all children, regardless of what church they or their parents do or do not belong to."

A broad smile came across her face, and she responded, "I can hardly wait until you have your Sunday school! You will let me know? My name is Cathy."

"Hello, Cathy," I said, "I'll be on the steps of the church at the same time next Sunday and then I can tell you when we'll be starting our Sunday school. "Will you come here so I can tell you? "I asked.

"I'll be here," she replied and then went skipping down the block.

We made plans to begin our first church school in two weeks. We had to choose lesson materials and secure teachers. When the next Sunday afternoon arrived, I found Cathy waiting for me by the church gates.

"I told you I'd be here, didn't I?" she beamed.

I found it hard to believe that my first contact with a child from these streets could be so easy. Cathy had brought her sister, who was two-years younger.

"This is my sister, Linda. She would like to come, too."

After asking about other children in their neighborhood, I unlocked the church door, and we went in.

"Where are you going to have Sunday school?" the girls wanted to know as they followed me inside. "The other preacher had his downstairs."

Since I had permission from the Hungarian pastor to use the upper sanctuary, I told them it would be in the sanctuary and showed them what that was like. The girls seemed pleased as they left through the big, wide front doors.

Our first Sunday school session was attended by 15 children, all contacts having been made through Cathy and her friends on her block. News gets around quickly in city blocks and goes the distance of a child's travels. There were children from 10th Street and 12th Street on that first Sunday afternoon.

For the next few months the attendance remained between 16 and 20 children, with new ones coming in and others dropping out. We made house calls on the families of the children who came and discovered the kinds of lives these East Side children lived. Most were white but represented a variety of nationalities and included two or three Puerto Rican children who lived in a dilapidated brownstone on the block.

19

A Boy Named Junior

One day I was passing out flyers on Third Avenue concerning a series of meetings we were conducting at the church, when a young African-American boy walked up to me, smiled and asked, "Whatcha passing out there? May I have one?" I gave him one, and he walked toward the corner.

In a moment he came back, looked up at me and said, "You look like a preacher. Are you a preacher? They don't usually pass out things like that. Are you really a preacher?"

I replied that I was and told him our church was on 11th Street.

"Oh, that's by where I go to school now, P.S. 19. It's over on 2nd Avenue."

I asked him where he went to church.

"Oh, we don't go anywhere, but, I'd like to go. Can I come to your church?"

"Yes, you can come," I replied. "Our Sunday school starts at 2:30 on Sunday afternoon and all children are welcome."

"Oh! I have two brothers and a sister. Could you come and talk to my mother? Maybe they could come, too."

I agreed to talk to his mother and went with him to the slum hotel where he lived above a large store that specialized in work clothes. The building actually consisted of three brownstones that had been connected. We entered from a side street and walked up a narrow set of stairs.

At the top of the stairs, in a cubbyhole, sat a fat black man at a small desk with a telephone. He looked at me with an expression of utter contempt, and then turned to the boy and with a gruff voice said, "Stop running in and out. I thought you were a nice boy."

The smile left the boy's face, and with a sullen look he replied, "Yes, Sir."

Then he went on to say, "This man is a preacher, and I want him to see my mother."

With that, the look on the man's face suddenly softened as he muttered something I did not understand. Then the boy bounded down the dark hallway, saying, "Come on, I'll show you where I live. You'll get lost if I don't."

A passageway had been cut through each building, and this was the only access from the narrow stairs to each of the four upper floors. There were four one- or two-room units on each floor. Each floor shared a single toilet.

We went through the passageway to the third building and climbed three flights of stairs. As I reached the hallway at the top, the boy was already beyond an open doorway across the hall talking a mile a minute to his mother, who was stirring something in a pot on a gas stove.

The woman's appearance on that day was virtually the same as it has been the hundreds of times I have seen her since. Her skin was light brown. Her slightly grayish hair was combed straight back from the sides of her head and stuck out in the back as though the combing had not been completed. She was dressed in nondescript, shabby clothes.

"Come in," she said, after hesitating for a minute, as though she was not sure what to do with my unexpected appearance in her home.

As I walked through the open doorway and looked around, my first inclination was to turn around and get out of this horrible place as fast as I could. I thought, *Do people actually live here?* I was fearful of some incredible danger lurking in one of the dark hallways in this building situated on a corner where murder, rape, and robberies have occurred with surprising frequency. Here, though, I was with a small eight-year-old boy with pleading eyes who wanted to go to Sunday school.

It seemed surreal that I should be in these strange surroundings, talking to this woman about her son; but I soon realized I must be on friendly ground. This was an interior room, without windows, and the only light in the room came from one bare overhead bulb.

Another one of my first thoughts was that the other room must be better than this, for the city would surely not permit occupancy of such a place as this. How mistaken I was.

As the woman turned down the flame under the pot, I could see that their supper would be rice and beans. She opened the refrigerator to return a milk carton, and the white light from inside revealed empty shelves, except for a few containers with unrecognizable contents, some pork fat and the lone milk carton.

Well, at least they have a refrigerator, I thought. The other furnishings in the room consisted of a metal-topped table and two chairs. She offered me one of the chairs, and I gladly sat down, feeling winded from climbing the many stairs behind the fleet-footed boy.

"I really want my children to go to Sunday school," she said, "but I just don't know of any close by." The churches where she had previously sent her children were in the Bronx, and she could not afford the carfare to get them there. They had moved from the Bronx three months ago, and the only people she knew were the other mothers in the building with children the ages of hers.

At this she moved from the stove, brushing the left side of her head with her hand, as though she had a headache, a gesture that I would come to see her do many times. She asked me if I would like to go sit in the other room.

As I entered the room, I saw that there were only three pieces of furniture there—an old dresser and two double beds, upon one of which a small boy was sleeping. There was a window on one side of the room and a brick wall beyond it, letting in very little light. The six-foot-square opening turned out to be an inside air passage between buildings and the only source of outside air in these two rooms. Although it was mid-afternoon on a bright late spring day, another bare bulb provided the only real light in the room.

I asked if it would be all right to bring in the chair that I had been sitting on. At that, the smiling boy jumped up from the bed where he had been sitting and said, "I'll get it for you."

Beside the eight-year-old, there was an older boy, a sister, and a younger brother (the one who was sleeping) in the home. "My children all need to be in Sunday school. Can they all come?" the mother asked.

"Oh, of course. They're all welcome to attend!" I replied eagerly. After getting their names, ages, and grades in school and chatting briefly, I said good-bye to the boy's mother.

I discovered that the boy who had led me to this apartment was called "Junior."

"You can't find your way out," Junior said. "I'll have to show you the way."

I followed him out, but, as a boy always does, he ran ahead. On the passageway I made a wrong turn to another hallway and came back to the passageway confused. As I caught sight of Junior coming around a corner, he said, "I told you you'd get lost."

"I'm glad you're here to show me the way out," I replied very sincerely.

Back on the street, Junior was all smiles and assured me, "Yes, I will be there next Sunday, Brother Frey." I had told him that "Brother Frey" is what others called me.

20
A Child Will Lead Them

Since that meeting was early in the week, I was impatient until the next Sunday afternoon. I had discovered that some of the children seemed to have trouble remembering addresses and tended to lose sight of times and dates.

For many of these City children, the present day, whatever it is, is important. Yesterday is totally forgotten, and they don't really want to think about tomorrow before it arrives. So many potentially great tomorrows become just another dreary today with hopes for fun and enjoyment smothered by the crises of today.

However, my concern about Junior's family proved to be unwarranted. Shortly before 2:30 on Sunday afternoon, as I stood by the gate outside the church's street-level basement, I spotted Junior leading his sister and two brothers. The children were neat and clean and fairly well dressed.

I soon learned their names. The girl was named Doris, but they called her Gail. The older brother was named Robert but was called either Bobby or Willie. The younger brother, Michael, was called Mike.

These were the first African-American children in our Sunday school, as most came from the surrounding blocks, whose residents were almost exclusively white. Many of the children were from families who had lived in those blocks for two or three generations. In fact, one did not really "belong" there until he or she had lived there a decade or two.

While I was pleased with the progress of our church school, I was wondering what would happen when our first black children came. When Junior and his three siblings entered, there was little stir. Some of the other children turned and looked at them when they came in, but then returned their attention to whatever was occupying them previously.

The adjustment was good and normal, and everybody was a little surprised at Bobby because he had been building a reputation on the street as a fighter. This "rep" Bobby zealously guarded, but at least he had not yet created a reaction among the white children on this block. None of them, as yet, had had a fight with him.

Junior was a smiling boy who seemed interested in everything, but his inquisitiveness was never cloying. It seemed always to be in the right place and time. It was a pleasure to answer his inquiries.

For a few Sundays, attendance remained at about 25. It was difficult to find enough teachers. Mrs. Frey and I asked several gifted young people with whom we were acquainted to come and help us, but they all turned down the opportunity for one reason or another.

This turned out to be one of the most difficult aspects of children's work in New York City—finding able and dedicated people willing to give their time on a regular basis. For a day or two, yes, but for a year or two is out of the question. "Too busy" is always the excuse. There seems to be time for all kinds of adult religious activities, but no time for children.

One Sunday afternoon, Junior approached me and asked if anyone else from his building could come to Sunday school. "Of course," I replied. "We would be happy to have them." I recognized, too, that many children generally will not go to a church unless they are convinced that they are welcome.

I told Junior that the next evening we could visit his friends together. We called on the MacDonald family who had five girls. As soon as I had been introduced, Junior smiled, said good-bye and was gone.

Junior was a "different" kind of boy. In appearance, he was lanky and tall for his age. He had close-cropped hair above a round face with a small protruding chin. What set him apart was not his appearance, but his unchanging temperament. Some might call him a dull person, always predictable, but to me he and Cathy represented my greatest "opportunities."

With Junior it was an opportunity to shape, mold, and direct a life.

With Cathy it was an opportunity to provide needed instruction concerning faith and help to provide direction along the path of life.

For the next eight years, Helen and I would do just that for these two youngsters and many other children from this and other neighborhoods. Our work among the needy children of the Lower East Side and other parts of New York City had begun.

21
Starting A Camp Ministry

It was during the first week of June 1958, when I spotted the father of Antonio, one of the children we were working with, on the street near the church. He was his usual self—bleary eyed but alert to the happenings of the block as he leaned against a light post, a beer in one hand and a cigarette in the other. When he saw me walking down the street, he lifted the hand with the beer can as if to greet me, then dropped it to his side and with the hand holding the cigarette waved a greeting.

As I opened the church gates, he walked up and looked at me as if he wanted to talk. Fastening the open gate, I said, "Good morning."

"Hello, Brother Frey. My boy, Antonio, he'd like to go to camp. Do you have camp for kids in the summer?"

His question set me to thinking seriously. We had looked into the possibility before and had given up the thought because of the many problems involved. What about an existing camp? We obtained various camp brochures. The rates were $45 per camper per week. Like many of our children's parents, Antonio's father could not afford that with the wages he earned and the large stair-stepped brood of children he was trying to clothe and feed.

The help that the family received from welfare was meager because there was a man in the home. If he had not been there, the family would have received about double what they received for rent, clothing and other child support. Antonio's mother had been so upset with the welfare worker for suggesting that she would be better off without her husband that she had stormed out of the welfare office and declared, "I'm not going back!" They subsequently received minimal assistance for clothing and little else.

We pondered the possibility of starting a camp for all of our Sunday school kids. Inquiries revealed that none of them had ever been to a camp. When we confronted the difficulties of providing a camp experience, we thought maybe we should consider holding a daily vacation Bible school (DVBS) instead.

We could not get teachers. Everybody I asked told me they were too busy. One mother also pointed out that the children would have to cross a busy avenue to get to the DVBS each day and that would be too hazardous in the summertime. When schools are in session, there are policemen directing traffic at the corners, but not during summer vacation. The children were "prisoners" of their blocks unless accompanied by an adult.

Finally, we hit on the idea of combining camp and DVBS: a vacation Bible school in a camp setting. We felt it was just what the children needed, but where? After attempts to locate an available camp setting through advertising brought no responses, I remembered a camp in Old Bridge, New Jersey where I had previously attended a conference.

We drove out and discovered that no camp program was scheduled for that summer. The man in charge of the camp had taken ill, and no one else would take on the responsibility. "Could we rent the camp?" The response was positive. A small rental fee was agreed upon, and our first camp program was launched.

We had promises of counselors and a cook, but when the camp opened, we found that we had neither. Mrs. Brown, our Sunday school teacher—a large woman past middle age—and Helen were our only staff.

I had made arrangements to take the first week off from my job, but at the last minute my employer refused to give me the week off. Reluctantly, he did give me that Saturday off, the day we would take the children to the Old Bridge camp.

Despite difficulties that had arisen, we started the camp with optimism. We had 16 children with Mrs. Brown as counselor and Helen as cook, counselor, and day director. The girls stayed in the cabins while the boys stayed in a nine-room house, where I had a room and served as dorm counselor when I was there. I had to commute 40 miles to work, catching the 6:30 a.m. train to New York and would arrive back at camp at 8:30 in the evening.

Upon my return I would hurriedly eat supper, which Helen had ready for me, and then begin the evening agenda, including skit and talent night put on by the campers. Between events I would be informed of the problems of the day, which consisted mainly of fights. There must have been a dozen in just the first day!

A pattern emerged as the days wore on, and the name of that pattern was "Billy." Others were involved, too, but at least half of the fights involved Billy. I handled any serious disturbances, but what was I to do with Billy?

Late one warm, beautiful, moonlit evening, Billy and I had a long talk, sitting on logs out near the road where we wouldn't disturb the sleeping campers. At first, Billy could offer no explanation for his actions. He told me that he wanted to be good like his brother, Junior, who never got into trouble, but whenever somebody did something to him, he felt compelled to get back at them, and to do so instantly.

"What do they do to you?" I asked.

"Mostly it's words," he explained, "or kids won't play with me. And sometimes if I want the ball, they won't give it to me. And sometimes, they push me out of a game that I want to be in."

I asked him to tell me his story concerning each fight, in order. He corroborated everything that I had been told about the various incidents without being evasive, untruthful, or defensive. In his exasperation, he finally blurted out, "I'm going to start my own camp. The kids will play with me or they won't be allowed to come!"

Now I knew what was upsetting the boy. He was on the outside and wanted in. We had a long talk, and I was very eager to talk to the other campers about what I had learned from our conversation; however, I had a job to get to especially early the next morning. One of the storeowners had gone on vacation, and I needed to open the store. So, I gave what instructions I could to Helen and then left.

That day there were more fights to be settled, and Billy was involved again. In the evening we did our best to plead Billy's case with the other campers. Billy even apologized publicly for his bad behavior and made a special apology to the girls, especially to one named Annette, whose hair he had pulled very hard. Although she would not tell me, other girls told me that Annette had been in such pain that she had cried most of the afternoon.

Billy's public apology—which he had made at my suggestion—was quite a performance for an eleven-year-old boy. Although I was moved by it, Helen was skeptical, Mrs. Brown was doubtful, and Junior commented, "he's a faker. That's all an act to get on the good side of the girls."

I replied, "Junior, are you trying to ruin your brother's attempt to make things right?"

"Naw," he said. "I just want him to be good, but he likes to be bad. He could be different if he wanted to."

I had suspected a possible scheme behind Billy's public apology, but greatly admired the performance. It had been done with great skill. He did end up on the good side of the girls, and his behavior was greatly improved. There was actually nothing bad to report on the last two days of camp. The kids stopped fighting each other and started playing together.

I have read a great deal about the need for a pecking order to be established among children, but I have discovered that this theory does not entirely stand up in a short-term camp situation. Long-standing feuds and a striving for preeminence and dominance might be the case when dealing with the interaction of children for longer periods of time. In the short time span of camp, however, the children's minds are too much on the fun of the moment and most fights are very transitory in nature.

Billy was a perpetual fighter and his brother, Junior, was his only stabilizer. Junior had stepped in to stop so many fights that he, too, was getting on the outs with the rest of the campers. When he realized this was happening, he stopped being an umpire between his older brother and the others. When Billy saw that occurring, he stopped fighting and sat on the sidelines watching the fun. Soon the campers were making up with him.

So, the final two days of camp were "heavenly." I could detect a very different atmosphere when I returned to camp from work each evening.

I have discovered in ministry that people's actions, reactions, and attitudes have a definite influence on places and things. By the final two days of camp, the children had become accustomed to the nature of a camp

111

program and were wholeheartedly participating in the various activities.

Billy did become a member of the "team." He became a happy, normal boy by the end, but it had been a hard, torturous journey for Sister Brown and Helen, who had carried the load during the daytime, and for me as I relieved them for the evenings. Our ultimate success, however, kept us open to the prospect of continuing and expanding our camp programs in ensuing years.

22
The Camp Ministry Grows

We continued to rent the Old Bridge facilities for two more years as the camp program grew and matured. Then, in 1961, we moved our camp program to a lovely spot in the Catskill Mountains, with rolling fields and a small lake, where the atmosphere was dry and healthy and the buildings were adequate for our needs at the time.

We reached out to the slowly growing list of our ministry's supporters for financial help with the costs of the camp and launched an annual fund-raising dinner for that purpose. Soon it became apparent that we would need our own camp facilities, and an 86-acre piece of property became available in the Taconic Mountain Range near Stephentown, New York. It was a place of rolling hills and fields, a view of mountains and pine trees and included an old, but well-built farmhouse. With a down payment of $1,000, the purchase was made in the fall of 1962.

The following year had its unique mixture of calamities and blessings. In the spring of 1963 we began renovating the property. An uncompleted porch was removed from the house, an old barn was leveled, old farm machinery was removed, heavy overgrowth was removed from the roadway near the house, and the right-of-way was cleared for the power lines. The summer camp program was limited to short periods with small groups of children because of an unsatisfactory water supply, and it became obvious we would need to have a well drilled.

In late July, Helen and I drove from the camp to New York City with our station wagon loaded with girls. Although we were tired, after delivering the campers to their various homes and destinations on the lower east side of Manhattan, we started the 150-mile trip back to camp late at night.

With Helen at the wheel, we drove on, despite our fatigue, as we were anxious to complete various unfinished tasks at camp the next day. On the Taconic Parkway, Helen fell asleep and drove off the road into a tree. The station wagon was demolished, and we were hospitalized in Poughkeepsie, N.Y., with significant injuries, but we were grateful to God for sparing our lives. After our release from the hospital we spent some weeks recuperating at the home of Helen's family in Albion, N.Y. before returning to our normal routine (at a greatly reduced pace) in New York City.

* * * * * *

Camp Activities

It is ofen said that a camp is only as good as its food. So with this concept, we made a special effort to serve three good meals each day. The campers ate heartily, and didn't seem to miss the junk food they were familiar with in the City.

Daily activities varied, but time was set aside each morning for Bible study and tent chores. In the afternoon, the kids would go to a lake to swim or boat. In the evening, they played softball or other outside games until dark.

Often in the evening, a special activity by some of the campers would be scheduled. On another evening, there would be perhaps singing and learning new camp songs, which the kids enjoyed. One treat was to take the campers to a country story in Vermont, a short distance from camp. On Sundays, we took the kids to a local church for the morning service, where they were welcomed with friendly smiles and handshakes.

One of the most memorable experiences at Camp was the bonfire on the last night. The boys would gather long sticks and sharpen the ends for roasting marshmallows. We would sing popular camp songs, including KUM BA YAH, DO LORD, PEACE LIKE A RIVER, JESUS LOVES ME, and others. Everyone joined in with great gusto. Then Marvin would speak words of love and hope to these special young-sters who were entrusted to our care for a very meaningful experience in their lives. A favorite Scripture verse would be read, followed by a prayer and the Lord's Prayer in unison.

When the time came to leave camp and return to the noisy city, the campers naturally resisted. Summer camp had opened up a whole new world for them, and they would think about the fun they had at camp for years to come.

Taking New York City kids away from their familiar sur-roundings was a life-changing experience. Many decisions for Christ were made in those twenty-six years, and it is a thrill to be in touch with some parents even today, who are living for Christ and leading their children to faith in Christ.

Marvin's philosophy about summer camp versus min-istry on the streets of New York City spoke loud and clear: One week at summer camp, he believed, was the equivalent of one year's ministry in New York City.

23
Popular Choruses Sung Today

Twenty of most sung choruses today with Copyright dates. Also on CD.

Alleluia, 1973

Blessing and Honor and Glory, 1977

Do Lord, 1977

He Is Lord, 1977

He Showed Me His Hands, 1977

He's All I Need, 1974

I Have Decided To Follow Jesus, 1983

I Have A Jubilee Down In My Heart, 1977

I Know It Was The Blood, 1977

I Love Him For He Is Mine, 1977

Isn't He Wonderful, 1973

I've Got Peace Like A River, 1977

Kum Ba Yah, 1936

Lord Make Us One, 1977

Oh The Blood of Jesus, 1977

Praise Him In The Morning, 1977

The Move Is On, 1977

This Is My Commandment, 1977

We'll Give The Glory To Jesus, 1977

With Healing In His Wings, 1978

Marvin V. Frey composed nearly three hundred songs with original manuscripts. During his life, he published three songs books:

From the Foreword of *The First Hearing Of The Songs and Music of Marvin Frey*:

"God has given my friend Rev. Marvin Frey a gift of writing songs-both words and music-that people find easy to remember and enjoy singing again and again.

In this unique compilation you will find, I know, some of your favorites, which you have sung and enjoyed for years but were not aware who had written them. Along with these you will find some of his newer creations that I feel sure will bless you greatly and are destined to become added favorites in the singing treasury of the Christian Church.

'Sing' cerely yours,

Dr. Alfred B. Smith,
Originator and Founder of Singspiration."

24

How The Choruses Were Inspired

I HAVE DECIDED TO FOLLOW JESUS
Words by Marvin V. Frey
Copyright ©1983 by Marvin V. Frey

I have decided to follow Jesus, (repeat)
I have decided to follow Jesus,
No turning back, no turning back.

Though no one join me, still I will follow; (repeat)
Though no one join me, still I will follow;
No turning back, no turning back.

In 1943 while conducting evangelistic services at the Highland Park Church of The Open Bible, in the meat-packing town of Ottumwa, Iowa, a large burly man responded to the invitation to accept Christ as his Savior. As this man, under the Holy Spirit's convicting power went forward to the altar, tears streamed down his cheeks, as he buried Reverend Frey's hand in his. With strong conviction he said, "I have decided to follow Jesus." The next night his wife and children accepted Christ as Savior.

When Marvin was leaving the church parking lot, the words flowed from the Holy Spirit, "no turning back."

"ISN'T HE WONDERFUL"

Isn't He wonderful, wonderful, wonderful,
Isn't Jesus my Lord, wonderful;
Eyes have seen, ears have heard,
It's recorded in God's word.
Isn't Jesus my Lord, wonderful?

Written in May 1947, at the Wings of Healing Temple, Portland, Oregon and inspired by a great sermon by Dr. Thomas Wyatt, at the opening spring convention on the text: I Corinthians 2:9 "The Unfolding Revelation of Jesus Christ." The original words were, 'eyes not seen, ears not heard, all's recorded in God's word. During the sermon, Dr. Wyatt exclaimed, "Isn't Jesus Wonderful." The song was sung over the national 180-station radio broadcast and it swept the country like wildfire.

In 1974, 27 years after the chorus was written, God answered Marvin's prayer with three verses that fit the chorus like a glove.

KUM BA YAH (Come By Here)

Come by here, my Lord, come by here,
Come by here, my Lord, come by here,
Come by here, my Lord, come by here,
O Lord, Come by here.

Kum ba yah, my Lord, kum ba yah,
Kum ba yah, my Lord, kum ba yah,
Kum ba yah, my Lord, kum ba yah,
O Lord, kum ba yah.

At age 18, I wrote the chorus, "Come By Here." While leading a children's group at a camp meeting in Centralia, Washington, a young boy named Robert Cunningham was converted. He sang the song all over the camp ground in his high, boyish voice. Additionally, the chorus traveled to the Belgian Congo with American missionaries, whose burden was for Angola. But at that time, Angola was closed to protestant missionaries. The missionaries worked among Angolan miners from Southeast Angola in Stanleyville and were on contract for three years. The chorus was first translated and sung in French, which was the language spoken by the missionaries. The missionaries visited the churches (about forty) that their converts had founded in Angola. They heard a translation of a chorus they taught in the Lu Valle dialect of Eastern Angola. Upon their return to America they sang this song in the Angolan language, the Lu Valle dialect as "Kum Ba Yah."

Both songs, "Come By Here" and "Kum Ba Yah" are registered in the Library of Congress, Washington, D.C.

HE IS LORD

Words and music by Marvin V. Frey
Copyright ©1977 by Marvin V. Frey

He is Lord; He is Lord;
He is risen from the dead, and He is Lord;
Every knee shall bow, every tongue confess
That Jesus Christ is Lord.

He is mine; He is mine;
He is Lord of all the earth, and He is mine;
Everywhere I go, this one thing I know,
That Jesus Christ is mine.

Introduced on Easter Sunday, 1952, at the Wings of Healing Temple, Portland, Oregon, where the composer was music director and pianist on the national ABC network broadcast. The chorus is based on Philippians 2:10-11, written over a period of three weeks, but I was not satisfied with how the tune began. By direct leading of the Holy Spirit, one hour before morning worship, the first three notes of *He is Lord* was composed. The chorus became popular immediately.

I'VE GOT PEACE LIKE A RIVER
Copyright ©1977 by Marvin V. Frey

I've got peace like a river, Peace like a river,
I've got peace like a river in my soul.
I've got peace like a river, Peace like a river,
I've got peace like a river in my soul.

I've got joy like a fountain, Joy like a fountain,
I've got joy like a fountain in my soul.
I've got joy like a fountain, Joy like a fountain,
I've got joy like a fountain in my soul.

I've got love like an ocean, Love like an ocean,
I've got love like an ocean in my soul.
I've got love like an ocean, Love like and ocean,
I've got love like an ocean in my soul.

Inspired by comments made by an evangelist during the mid-week service at the Wings of Healing Temple, Portland, Oregon in 1950. The chorus was introduced moments after it was composed. The second verse was written after the service. An idea for the third verse was suggested by a female student at the Portland Bible Institute. Pastors, evangelists and Christian workers from all over the nation came and returned to their churches and homes singing the choruses they heard and sang at the Portland Revival. Hence the widespread use of many of the choruses composed during my time as the musical director and pianist for the Wings of Healing broadcast.

I KNOW IT WAS THE BLOOD

I know it was the blood, I know it was the blood, I know it was the blood for me;

One day when I was lost, He died upon the cross, And I know it was the blood for me.

Composed publicly before 5,000 people at Angelus Temple, Los Angeles, California in October 1938, where the famed evangelist, Aimee Semple McPherson was founder and pastor. The song was a take-off on her sermon, "The Blood of Jesus."

LORD MAKE US ONE

Lord make us one, Lord make us one, Lord, make us one
everywhere;
Lord make us one, Lord make us one, Lord, make us one
everywhere.

One in Jesus' blood.
One in the Holy Ghost.
One in winning souls.

Was composed from a theme suggested by Rev. Emma Cotton, well-known African American evangelist in Southern California. It was the theme chorus for the 33rd anniversary revival at Angelus Temple, October 1939. Rev. Emma Cotton was the evangelist and Rev. Marvin V. Frey was musical evangelist and pianist.

25
Our Miracle Home

Ode to Our New Home

To my husband, Marvin, February 14, 1968
by Helen Frey

The clock strikes twelve, the years have passed,
The dream of our life has come at last.
We couldn't see how Tho' hope kept alive
Faith in our lovely and wonderful Lord.

As we sit by the hearth, our hearts all aglow,
Counting our blessings, 'Tis a miracle, we know!
May our home be a witness to all who pass by,
That Christ is the Saviour, His love will not die.
May the love that we share emit through this home,

To tell the great love The Father hath shown.

26
Our Lifetime Dream—Trip to Israel

Through a generous gift from one of Marvin's aunts, we were able to take a trip to Israel. This desire was in Marvin's heart and mind since his youth. The big day arrived and on March 22, 1985, we departed from New York City, and with a stop-over in London, landed safely the next night at Tel Aviv airport. Arrangements were made prior to departing, for a responsible Israeli to meet us and take us to our hotel late at night.

The next day we flew via El Al plane to Cairo for three interesting days. With our tour guide we crossed the Nile River at its widest, five miles. The famous river is 4,050 miles long and because of rich sediment deposits, Northern Egypt is one of the most fertile regions in the world. We viewed the Avenue of the Sphinx at Luxor, rode on camels wearing Egyptian garb. One of the most awesome sights was seeing the Hall of Columns at Karnak covered with hieroglyphics, and a mound of bricks inside the main gate. One day was spent at the Valley of the Kings, the tomb of King Tut, and the tomb of Ramses. The sights were incredible; however, our hearts were heavy as we saw the poverty, especially among children whose lifestyle is to beg from tourists in their midst.

From Egypt we returned to Israel and the West Bank for several days' visit. Before our trip, we made contact with two schools on the West Bank: Hope Secondary School, whose director is Rev. Solomon Nour and Bethlehem Bible College with president, Dr. Bishara Awad. We were privileged to be invited as guests at Hope Secondary School for our stay in Israel. Marvin spoke to the attentive boys and girls at this school. What a joy it was to share the gospel with the student body and staff at Bethlehem Bible College.

Another dear man of God, Rev. Jonathan Esawi, pastor of The Church of God on the West Bank, had a Saturday Sunday school which we visited. What a privilege and blessing it was to fellowship with these true, humble servants of God, in a land with many difficulties and daily challenges. Since 1985 we have supported these men with prayers and finances, and thank God for their faithfulness.

The people of Israel are friendly, and have a sense of pride about their land. On a walk one day near Hope Secondary School we noticed a narrow path leading downward, and discovered it was the Valley of Elah, the place where David overtook and killed the giant, Goliath. Suddenly the reality of where we were transfixed us; we were standing on 'holy ground,' where Jesus walked with his disciples and where he performed many miracles.

The Bible stories we learned as children seemed to come alive with new and greater meaning. We were overwhelmed with the reality that we were walking right where Jesus walked.

Our trip was planned to include two traditional religious holy days: Palm Sunday and Easter. Palm Sunday was a clear, sunny day, ideal for the four-hour long procession down Via Dolorosa. The streets of Jerusalem were lined with boy scouts in their kaki uniforms and bright red hats, posed for pictures. Our eyes turned to one man's harem of several women en route to the parade. Marvin got his camera out, and suddenly one woman rushed forward to grab it, but unsuccessfully. He did get a picture with his camera guarded.

The spring season in Israel was bursting with flowers in full bloom. Beds of bright pink sweet peas covered the garden tomb of Lazarus in Bethany. In the distance on a hillside picturesque scene – a Bedouin Camp between Bethany and Jericho. One impressive experience was our invitation to visit the Church of The Ten Lepers in Borqin, by the pastor, who served us tea. The ten lepers were healed at this Church, but only one leper, Naaman, went back and thanked God for healing him. In the distance we saw the Valley of Megiddo, site of biblical Armageddon, and the Church of the Nativity at Manger Square in Bethlehem.

Rev. Esawi took us on a two-day tour to the Sea of Galilee and other biblical sites, where large tour groups could not go because of narrow, winding roads. We stayed overnight with Rev. Esawi's parents and learned much about the Israeli culture, while sensing the threat of danger that surrounded them.

Easter Sunday, we attended the first Sunrise Service at the Garden Tomb with some minister friends. There was a large crowd at this English service, conducted by an English Chaplain. The traditional Easter hymns were sung, and then to our surprise, Marvin's song, "He Is Lord." We went back later in order to meet the Chaplain. Later in the day we met several friends and had wonderful fellowship. What a glorious Easter!

Departing from Israel after a wonderful visit, we flew to Athens, Greece for two days' visit. The Acropolis was closed due to a strike minutes before our arrival. So we decided to tour Paul's missionary journeys at Old Corinth. The next night we crossed the Mediterranean Sea on a large ship headed for Rome where we spent three days. Then to Venice by boat, with a man, our taxi, taking our luggage on his back. The canals around Venice are fascinating, and the sunsets awesome. A brief visit to Milan to see the Church of

The Last Supper; the painting, 'The last Supper' was being restored, so only part of it was visible.

Of all the European countries, Switzerland is one of the cleanest and most picturesque. We stayed first in Berne, to view the bears, whence its name. Young people played chess and tic-tac-toe in Berne Square Saturday evening where parents and friends gathered for fun and food. Then on a train trip to Zermott, we viewed awesome sights ranging from plush green farmlands to familiar chalets, to cozy villages tucked in valleys between mountains. One day's trip took us by cog rail to the skiers paradise, the lofty Matterhorn, a gorgeous, sunny day making the skiers very happy. On Sunday we boarded a train to Zumiswald, to see the home where Marvin's grandmother was born. One could sense the pride of these residents by the impressively clean city and well-kept buildings. Standing tall was a white church with stained glass windows built in 1200 A.D. with a German tower and clock. What memories!

Our next country to visit for two days was France. The majestic Eiffel Tower rose 984 feet into the sky. One day spent at Notre Dame Cathedral with the rose windows, north and south, which Marvin caught on camera and used on the covers of two songbooks published in 1991. Sights at the famous Louvre were Mona Lisa, The Reapers, Christ at Emmaus (Rembrandt), and Whistler's Mother.

The last leg of our dream trip were spent in London. First we saw John Wesley's home, office, prayer closet, pulpit and grave site. Wesley's Chapel opened November 1, 1778, to continue work begun at the Foundry near this site in 1739. It was built to be the center of Methodist worship and tradition. We took a picture of a copy of Charles Wesley's original hymnbook. We viewed the Tabernacle of George

Whitfield, the tomb of David Livingstone at Westminster Abbey. Finally, we stood for hours by a high fence to view Buckingham Palace and the historic 'changing of the guard.'

The next day flying from London to New York brought us back to the real world and to our beloved home. The wealth of pictures taken on this dream trip have given us such joy and gratitude for this once in a lifetime experience.

27
A Trip Down Memory Lane

Reminiscences of Three Former Campers

What follows are the reminiscences of Joe Preston, Ted Hamczyk, and Miriam Gonzalez, as they share memories of growing up in New York City, and how the Children's Ministry helped shape their lives, even to this day. Writer and editor, Vicki T. deVries, interviewed these former campers who are now adults and who say they will never forget Marvin and Helen Frey and the impact they had on their lives.

Joe Preston
What was life like growing up in New York City for you and your peers?

As a kid, growing up in New York City afforded me a raw metropolitan experience, although I was not really aware that I was getting so much knowledge at the time. In addition, growing up in the downtown area of a lower income neighborhood didn't allow us the privilege of associating with richer families of better means; but we didn't realize we were poor because all of us were the same! We had nobody with whom to compare ourselves.

We were decent kids with decent values, and saw our own levels of less and more fortunate. This sometimes meant becoming tougher, both physically and mentally, to get along. In any case we endured our happiness and struggles, and found our own comfort level while always aware of the potential dangers. We did what we had to do to survive.

How did you first get involved with the Children's Ministry and with Brother and Sister Frey, as the kids called them?

I can honestly say I've known the Freys for as long as I can remember. They had already been involved with the older generation in the neighborhood, which included my brother. I would always see Brother Frey come to take the older kids to camp and always ask if I could go. He would smile and say that I would have to wait until I was 8 years old before I could go to camp. I would smile back and say, 'okay.' I kept asking until the year I was 8 and finally went to camp!

Going to camp with this ministry afforded us a cleaner lifestyle from playing in the dirty parks and mean City streets, which were mostly overcrowded and inhabited by drug dealers, prostitutes, and the homeless.

One of the most difficult situations I ever saw Brother Frey face was when one kid sneaked into one of the cars and became a stowaway just so he could go to camp. About halfway upstate he was discovered, and Brother Frey had to make the difficult decision whether to have the kid stay at camp, or bring him back to the city. The State's strict rule regarding the number of occupants at camp dictated the sad fact, that the boy would have to be taken back to his home.

What was a typical day at camp like?

A typical day at camp meant looking forward to a lot of fun with great meals and of course, Bible study, which was part of the backbone of the whole ministry.

It was presented in a fun and enjoyable way instead of being jammed down our throats. The Bible instruction was required in order to have fun, and everyone knew that; so we complied. It certainly was a positive influence as I reflect on it now.

There were always planned activities for the day with free time to do what we wanted. The camp property in Stephentown, New York offered large, open playing fields and woods for hiking and having fun exploring. We would hike, play ball, do chores around the camp for Brother Frey, and just relax. It wasn't always easy to keep restless kids involved in one particular subject for too long; so Brother and Sister Frey and the counselors did the best they could to entertain us.

One of our most enjoyable excursions was to go to the community lake and swim—something we did on an almost daily basis, depending on the weather. Sometimes we would beg to go and Brother Frey would give in and take us; whereas Sister Frey was more of the disciplinarian. Among the most 'dangerous' fun times were those trips to the lake or the local store when we would hang off the car bumpers or out of the windows. We flew over the bumps and loved it, like a roller-coaster ride. Brother Frey had fun and wanted us to have fun too!

In the evenings, we usually had a musical concert which was hosted by Brother Frey and his music, or a local musician who would come by. Getting involved with the local townsfolk became more interesting as I got older. Families who lived in Stephentown and attended the local church would invite us to their homes for social visits.

Going to camp was one of my favorite things, and when old enough, I was a junior counselor, then a senior counselor. When I came of driving age, Brother Frey taught me how to drive. One great challenge was driving 15 screaming city kids to camp, a three-hour drive, and back to New York City after camp.

How did music play a role in Joe's experience with the Freys?

Brother and Sister Frey played their own music, which removed the hard edge of the religious angle and made it enjoyable. Later in life, I realized that I was great friends with a master musician and songwriter. Since Brother Frey had written 'Come By Here' (Kum Ba Yah) when a young man, I was very proud that I knew him. As a young kid, I just enjoyed knowing them as Brother and Sister Frey.

As you grew older, what kind of involvement did you have with the ministry?

I started drifting away from yearly active involvement when I started attending The School of Visual Arts and having to work part-time. Intermittently, I would get involved, helping as much as I could, but not as much as before.

What did you learn that made a lasting impression on you?

I learned that there was more to life than just the inner-city. Through my acquaintance with the Freys, I was able to experience travel, country living, different foods, different types of people and values. Had it not been for the Freys, those wonderful childhood summers would have been spent on the dirty City streets, and in less-than-desirable public swimming pools and parks during the down-turned economic times in New York City during the '60's and '70's.

How would you describe the impact the Freys have made on your life?

Brother and Sister Frey were always a positive influence by setting an example of living a clean, generous, and selfless lifestyle. They gave so much of themselves to others without asking for anything in return. Their reward was seeing the children playing with happy faces and knowing they were giving them hope for the future, and hope in themselves to achieve good goals in life. The key ingredient that made all this possible was that God provided the acknowledgement from people who believed in their ministry through monetary donations, and volunteering their time. Brother and Sister Frey are two of the most unselfish people I have ever known.

I hope that someone who reads this Book will have the vision of opening a children's camp someday, and name it after them.

That would be the ultimate honor.

Down Memory Lane with The Freys, an article by Miriam Gonzalez

My family has known the Freys since before 1966 when I was born. When I was about six years old, we moved to New Jersey. My older siblings have known the Freys for as long as I can remember, and to this present day I still send Sister Frey a Christmas card.

As a family, we didn't have much. I am one of 13 kids; so I had a lot of hand-me-downs, although to me they were as good as new. I often slept on the floor, but I didn't mind as long as we were all together. Sometimes we would go to bed extra early because we were hungry and this kept us out of our drunken stepfather's way.

When Miriam was asked about the children's ministry and summer camp, she replied:

For me, camp was truly an awesome experience. I thought, "wow, someone is taking me to camp, and all I have to do is listen to God's word and sing some songs?" I didn't realize that there was a bigger Hand at work until my later years. I wouldn't trade those times for anything.

My siblings and I would arrive before other campers, I think, because we lived the farthest away. The anticipation was always great. I loved the fresh smell of grass, that smell of the early morning dew, going to the tents. The sense that you can be among trees and find your way to a great adventure with singing and praising God as loud and long as you wanted, and it was okay.

At camp we all had some small chore to do, and received rewards either in the form of praise or some token on paper, which we were allowed to use to purchase candy at a canteen the Freys would set up. As a small child I was grateful, and could not understand that it was okay to buy something for myself. I have always, and still do, put others first, probably because my family has gone through so many ordeals. Simply put, 'we do for each other, or nothing at all.'

Given Marvin Frey's tremendous musical talent, how was music treated at the camp?

Music was our way of feeling like a team. Sometimes I felt a little silly when I would get consumed with the music. My family would make fun of me, but Brother Frey would always take charge and everything would be all right. I didn't realize how talented he was because I was young, but I know I enjoyed it.

After summer camp was over, the Freys did not simply forget Miriam and her large family. To the contrary, Miriam explains.

Brother and Sister Frey would always come to see us before Christmas to bring us stockings full of fruit, candy, brownies, nuts, and a little book about God's miracles. We loved them for doing this because food was scarce around Christmas time. These goodie bags were sometimes our only Christmas gift. How grateful I felt to receive it. I thanked God for helping Brother and Sister Frey make this visit, not only to our family in New Jersey, but to many families in New York City. I will always remember how warm and loved they made me feel, especially at Christmas time.

When asked what kind of legacy Brother and Sister Frey left to Miriam and the other children to whom they ministered over the years, she replied:

Brother and Sister Frey had big hearts for everyone. They understood that I was born into this situation and hadn't asked to be underprivileged. They showed me that I should be proud to be one of God's children and to know that I am loved by God. I can have peace in the world, and life has so much to offer if we will look and live. I was important in God's eyes, irregardless of my background or nationality.

The Freys taught me how to believe in God, in myself, and in my family, and how strong a family can be when we are all together. We have to make a choice to be good. If it were not for the Freys I would not have that total sense of security in knowing that God is always with me and that things happen for a reason.

I thank God that my family had the opportunity to know Brother and Sister Frey, and I thank them from the bottom of my heart for their influence in shaping who I am and who I have become.

Is there any greater legacy that one can leave another, especially as that influence draws others to find peace with

God? Such is the legacy of Marvin and Helen Frey, which shall last through eternity.

The Testimony of Ted Hamczyk

When I thought about what to write concerning how I feel about Brother Frey's Ministry and his music, I decided the best way to approach this is through a poem called 'Father.'

Father

When we are born, we have no choice of parents;
We are left with what God wants for us.
But somewhere between our birth and our death,
God grants us with a parent who loves us unconditionally;
Though not of blood, but love.

Brother Frey was a Father to me.
I guess that I was the Son that he couldn't have.
He nurtured and taught me about the meaning of life.
He never preached at me.
He always filled me with love.
We spoke for countless hours
About his dreams, his heart,
And his absolute devotion to God.
He was, and still is my hero.
I know that I disappointed him,
But he was big enough to forgive me.
He loved me as I am,
And I know that once again,
Someday I will touch his face,
And I will tell him:
'Father, I love you.'

To start at the beginning, I was born January 5, 1955, the seventh child of immigrant parents who arrived on Ellis Island in October 1950. We didn't have a lot; we were poor but we had each other. My parents were together until my father died in 1980; my Mom is still living.

I became aware of a Sunday School in the early 60's, when I was six or seven years old. Just a few blocks from where I grew up 1 met the Freys, who invited me to their Sunday School. So one Sunday I went and enjoyed this new experience.

My parents were Catholics, and that is the way I was brought up. The vivid memories I have of growing up were of stolen, abandoned cars on the street, of drug dealers and users, prostitutes, and street crime. Over the years the scene changed, when the Freys and their ministry brought a 'ray of hope' to 11th Street, where I was brought up.

Another 'ray of hope' came with the start of Summer Camp, away from the dirty, noisy City, into the clean, countryside for a week. This was the big and most important event of the year.

I can't help but believe that a lot of the success stories resulted in large part from the ministry and involvement of the Freys. I remember a kid, Robert, who lived on my street, one of eleven siblings, who attended camp. He grew up, got a job as a bank clerk, then a loan officer, followed by a chief loan officer, and finally a bank manager. For someone in my neighborhood to achieve such success, is unbelievably outstanding.

One of the fondest memories I have is of a lovely woman, Sister Benson, who cooked three meals a day for us hungry campers. The food was nutritious and good, and three meals a day were not the customary regimen of the City kids.

Camp gave me an opportunity to learn about the Lord. One of those ways was through music and a Bible story. A talented musician from the area, Bob Hebler and his family came and sang, and led the campers in lively songs. There was no 'fire and brimstone' preaching, but Bible truths were told clearly, without compromise, but in love.

Since Brother Frey was an accomplished musician, he understood the value of music to a New York City kid. He taught many songs he had written, which were faith-based, and easy tunes they could learn readily. What fun, and what an important experience.

Activities at the Camp were varied. Cherry Plain was a local park with a lake where we could boat, fish, or swim. Nature hikes, baseball, volley ball, all helped us to forget the grime and crime of City life.

One camp session when I was a junior counselor, some campers from Brooklyn knew there was fruit in the basement of the staff house, and decided to help themselves one night. One might choose to punish them, but Brother Frey felt this could be a 'learning experience.' There was an understanding that these things were there for them, but to steal them was not an option. All they needed to do was ask. Yes, Brother Frey had much patience, but clearly a lesson was learned.

As I grew older there developed a special comradery between Brother Frey and me. We took day trips driving many miles and talking about life issues, religion, politics, history and events in each of our lives. It was a father/son relationship; no judgment, just heart to heart talks. How memorable to me.

In conclusion, I am grateful to be married for thirty-two years to the same woman. My growth/development professionally has been greatly affected by the Freys ministry and influence. I am a happy person with a happy family, a wonderful wife and children, due in large part to the Freys involvement in me, and my involvement in their lives and ministry.

"GIFTS"

The Gift of our Lord Jesus Christ...
Comes not from asking...
But in the belief in Him...
That He will provide.

So many crave the dollar,
And spend their lives to achieve that end!
But they all just end up empty...
Without the blessings that only God can send.

You see...the birds in the forest,
Seek no fortune or fame!
But God will always provide for them.
And all of this in Jesus' Name.

It's in the Name of Jesus
That comfort can be sought.
And it's a comfort that lasts forever...
A comfort that can't be bought.

It's all in the Name of Jesus,
But the keys to His kingdom remain,
And none shall ever possess it...
'Lest it's asked for in Jesus' Name.

* * *

To honor Sister Frey
From Ted Hamczyk 7/07

28

Photo Gallery

Revival Choruses

1938
EVANGELIST MARVIN VIRGIL FREY

THEME CHORUS

Come By Here - Words & Music by Marvin V. Frey

1 Come by here, Lord, come by here,
Come by here, Lord, come by here,
Come by here, Lord, come by here,
   Oh, Lord, come by here.

2 Somebody needs salvation, Lord; Come by here,

3 Somebody needs a healing Lord, Come by here,

4 Somebody needs the Holy Ghost, Come by here,

**1957–Camp at Old Bridge, New Jersey, counselor
Elizabeth Peterson**

**1968–William Marshall guest violinist, camp, with
Boston Symphony Orchestra**

**1969—Helen plays piano at Sunday School,
E. 11th St. Church, New York City**

**1973—
Campers line
up for lunch,
Stephentown,
New York**

1979–Campers play softball, Stephentown, New York

1980–Bowling Team, Lower East Side, New York City

1980's–Brother Frey with boys from a Block Club on the Lower East Side of Manhattan. They were his joy and delight.

1980–11th St. Block Club Girls Party, with Bro. Frey's shirts

1980–Annual Dinner with guest singer, Alfred Smith, founder, Singspiration

1981–Joe Preston graduates from The School of Visual Arts, New York City

**1982–Trophies given to softball team members,
Annual Dinner**

**1984–3rd Street Block Club, sledding in
Van Cortlandt Park, New York City**

1985–Easter Sunday on West Bank, Israel, with friends

1986–13th Street Ball Team in uniform

1986–Unity Center Christmas Party, Brooklyn, New York

1987–softball teams ready to play, field #8 at 10th St. and FDR Dr.

1988–Dr. Gordon Anderson presents to Marvin and Helen award for 50 years ministry as evangelist, pastor, songwriter, youth director

1995–Six members, Board of Trustees, of Children's Fund of New York, Inc.

**1998–Extended family
Esther and Tom Gajtkowski
with Helen**

**1998–Historical marker
near gravesite of
Marvin Frey, 1998,
West Barre, New York**

**2001–
Rev. and Mrs. Richard Del Rio,
pastor of Abounding Grace
Ministries, New York City**

2001–Helen and Lou Codella with softball team at
10th St. and FDR Drive, New York City

2001–Mantel of Children's New York ministry,
handed over to Rev. Del Rio (right), pastor,
Abounding Grace Ministries, New York City

2001—Trophies from Rev. Frey's memorabilia given to the Del Rio brothers for their fine leadership of softball games, New York City

2007—Rev. Stephen Clark, Vice President for Development for The Orchard Foundation, and administrator for the "Marvin and Helen Frey Scholarship Fund"

"Unheralded Songwriter"
Charisma Magazine, 1985

**2003–Niece, Joyce Bradley and Marilynne Emmons are
hostesses at Helen's 80th birthday party**

29

Bethel Gospel Association/The Children's Fund Of New York, Inc.

This ministry to needy New York City children and youth began in 1956. In 1962 the Children's Fund of New York, a New York City agency of The Bethel Gospel Association/Children's Fund of New York, Inc. was organized under the Laws of the State of New York.

This has been a continuous year-round ministry, with Athletic leagues starting in April through September, playing on turf, in a City ball park for over thirty years. Each week's game starts with a brief devotional, sharing God's word, and often leading to decisions to follow Christ.

Day trips to amusement parks and beaches in the New York City area, and most important, camp, comprise the summer activities. Winter sports are ice and roller skating, bowling, and weekly basketball in a rented gym at 9-2nd Avenue for twenty years.

Christmas parties have been a special treat for deprived children of Brooklyn: Bedford Stuyvesant and East New York Brooklyn, where 30,000 people live without one gospel church or mission. A Christmas party was also given on the Lower East Side of Manhattan. In all of these parties, gift bags were fillled with fruit, candy, nuts, brownie, and a scripture. To many, this would be their *only* Christmas gift.

It can truly be said that Marvin was a 'father figure' to hundreds, even thousands of boys who were without fathers. His heart of compassion always encouraged them to excel in school and sports, and they were highly motivated, some won scholarships to schools of higher learning.

Nearly all of the functions of The Children's Fund of New York, Inc. since its inception in 1956, (a totally 'faith' ministry), have been carried on with volunteers who have real concern and love for the less fortunate children of New York's Lower East Side. We were also blessed with a fine dedicated group of trustees, who gave freely of their time and talents. They worked with Marvin and Helen in developing and maintaining this much-needed ministry, sharing God's love with patience, steadfastness and grace.

For eight years we had the privilege of networking with a fine, strong evangelical church on East 7th Street, Abounding Grace Christian Ministries, with Reverend Richard Del Rio, pastor. Over these few years we have come to learn of the genuine love and compassion this family has shown to everyone they meet. Their witness reaches vast multitudes on the Lower East Side of New York City, and with God's help it will continue to minister to peoples needs for years to come.

At a special fellowship dinner in November 2001, after much prayer and discussion, the Del Rios and our Board of Trustees felt it was in God's plan to pass the Children's Fund of New York's ministry to the Del Rios, with God's blessing. In January 2002, Helen retired and relocated in western New York near her family and friends from her college days. With a sense of fulfillment and joy, we count our forty-five years sharing the good news of God's love to New York City's underprivileged children and youth a great honor and humbling experience.

30
Marvin and Helen Frey
Scholarship Endowment

In 2001, The Children's Fund of New York, Inc. established a Scholarship Endowment, a perpetual Fund which would provide worthy youths from the Lower East Side of New York an opportunity to pursue a Christian higher education. This would strengthen their Christian testimony as they become adults, and make the world a better place, and above all, provide for them a quality life.

In the past six years we are pleased that scholarships for fourteen worthy youths from the Lower East Side have been given. It is our prayer that this Fund will continue into, the next generation, and beyond.